The
BOOK of DARTS

The BOOK of DARTS

Paddy Whannel and Dana Hodgdon
Illustrated by Sig Purwin

Henry Regnery Company • Chicago

Library of Congress Cataloging in Publication Data

Whannel, Paddy.
    The book of darts.

    Bibliography.
    1. Darts (Game) I. Hodgdon, Dana H., joint
author. II. Title.
GV1565.W45 1976 794   76-6288
ISBN 0-8092-8136-8

Published by Henry Regnery Company
180 North Michigan Avenue, Chicago, Illinois 60601
Manufactured in the United States of America
Library of Congress Catalog Card Number: 76-6288
International Standard Book Number: 0-8092-8136-8

Published simultaneously in Canada by
Beaverbooks
953 Dillingham Road
Pickering, Ontario L1W 1Z7
Canada

This book is for:

Jeep, Alan, Gary, Charlie, Doc, Dick, Darryl,
John, Mel, Mike, Sonny, and Wren

Bill, Bill junior, and Dave

Ken and Lynn

Finnegan, Giles, and Young
Count Alexander de Lesseps
Paulette and Karen
Ron

Contents

Acknowledgments

Our thanks to Kay Whannel, Linda Henry, Nicole Taghert, Stanley Lowy, Tony Wood of *Darts World,* and Doris Williams of the *News of the World*.

Introduction

Those who frequent pubs cannot help being struck by the increasingly familiar sight of a dart board under a bright light in one corner of the room. Clustered round it will be a group of enthusiastic players, intense in their concentration. To the uninitiated they seem to speak a strange language of their own; the air will resound to the cries of "double top," "bed and breakfast," and "mugs away."

In its origins an English pub game, darts has in recent years gained considerable popularity in other countries, especially the United States. Throughout the country there exists a network of local leagues as well as regional and national associations. Tournaments are organized on a regional, national, and even international basis. British teams have visited America and American players have competed in championships in England, including the famous *News of the World* Championship, which has some 500,000 entrants, the finals being watched by an estimated 12,000 spectators.

There are various reasons for the popularity of darts. It is a social game and can be played by various numbers of people. Basically a pub game, it can be played in the home and by the whole family. Since the game depends upon skill and not upon strength, women can excel at it as well as men. The playing area takes up little space and the equipment is inexpensive. A set of darts can be purchased for as little as $4.00 and a good bristle board for about $30.00.

This book offers a general introduction to the world of darts. It describes the board and the various games that can be played, including the strategies involved. There are sections on technique, equipment, and darts mathematics. In the concluding chapters we offer some observations on the obscure origins of the game as well as such matters as etiquette and terminology.

Primarily aimed at the beginner, it also contains, we hope, some things of interest to the expert player.

1   **The Dart Board**

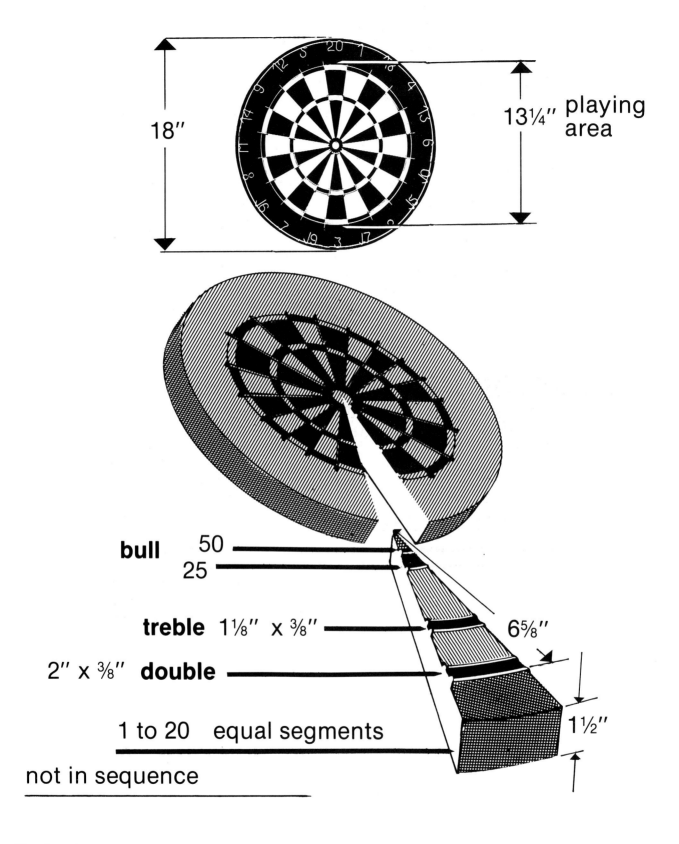

18″

13¼″ **playing area**

bull 50
25

treble 1⅛″ x ⅜″

2″ x ⅜″ **double**

6⅝″

1 to 20 equal segments

1½″

not in sequence

The Standard Board

A number of dart boards having very different designs have existed and, indeed, continue to be used in different parts of England. But the board that is most generally used and that has become the international standard is the clock, or London, board.

This board is divided by wires into 20 equal segments numbered 1 to 20—but not in that order. Two rings at the center represent the inner bull (scoring 50) and the outer bull (scoring 25). The board is further divided by a double ring and a treble ring, each three-eighths of an inch in width. A dart landing in the double ring scores double the number of that particular segment, while a dart landing in a treble triples the score. Thus a dart in a double 18 scores 36 and a dart in treble 18 scores 54. It will be seen that, contrary to the notion of the uninitiated, the highest score obtainable with one dart is 60 (i.e., treble 20), not the center bullseye. The maximum for one throw of three darts is, of course, 180 (i.e., all three darts in the treble 20).

The board measures 18 inches across, but the effective playing area is between the double rings and measures 13¼ inches across.

Setting Up the Board

The board should be fixed to the wall with the 20 segment uppermost and at a height of 5 feet, 8 inches from the *center* of the board to the floor.

The throwing line is 8 feet from the board—not from the wall. That distance is properly measured along the floor from a plumb line dropped from the center bull. In truth, in England the throwing distance has varied in different parts of the country. Visitors to the English pubs will have noticed the rubber mats supplied by brewers laid out before the dart board, marking off various distances up to 9 feet. However, with the growth of competitive darts the 8-foot throw has increasingly become the standard. The toe or throwing line (sometimes called the hockey line or simply "the hockey") must be clearly marked. In some cases it is raised slightly to prevent players from stepping over it.

The board must be well lit, ideally with an overhead light out of reach of the path of the darts but not too much at an angle to cast a shadow. The board should also be set up in an area away from doors or where casual passers-by are likely to walk into the flight path. Too often in the pub the board is set up between the bar and the lavatories, where the player concentrating on treble 20 comes in conflict with customers with more urgent needs in mind.

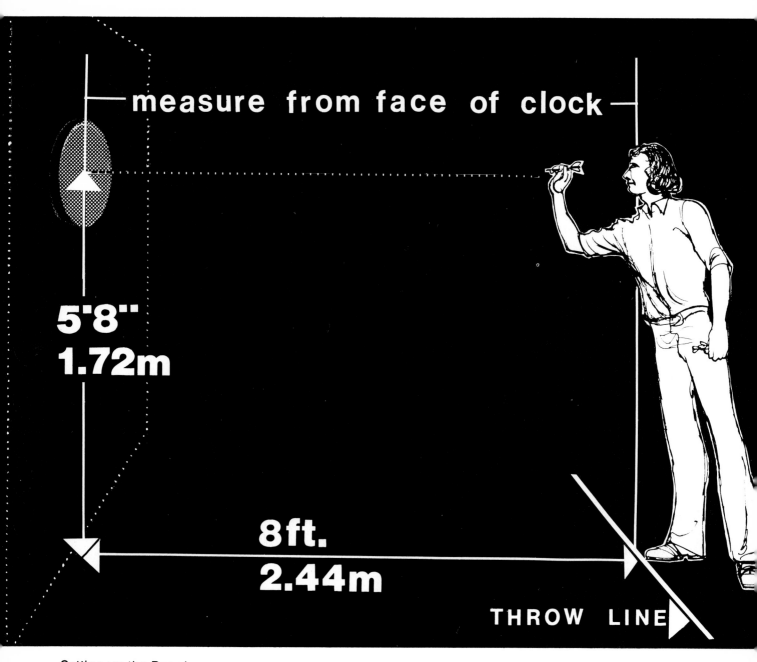

measure from face of clock

5'8"
1.72m

8ft.
2.44m

THROW LINE

Setting up the Board

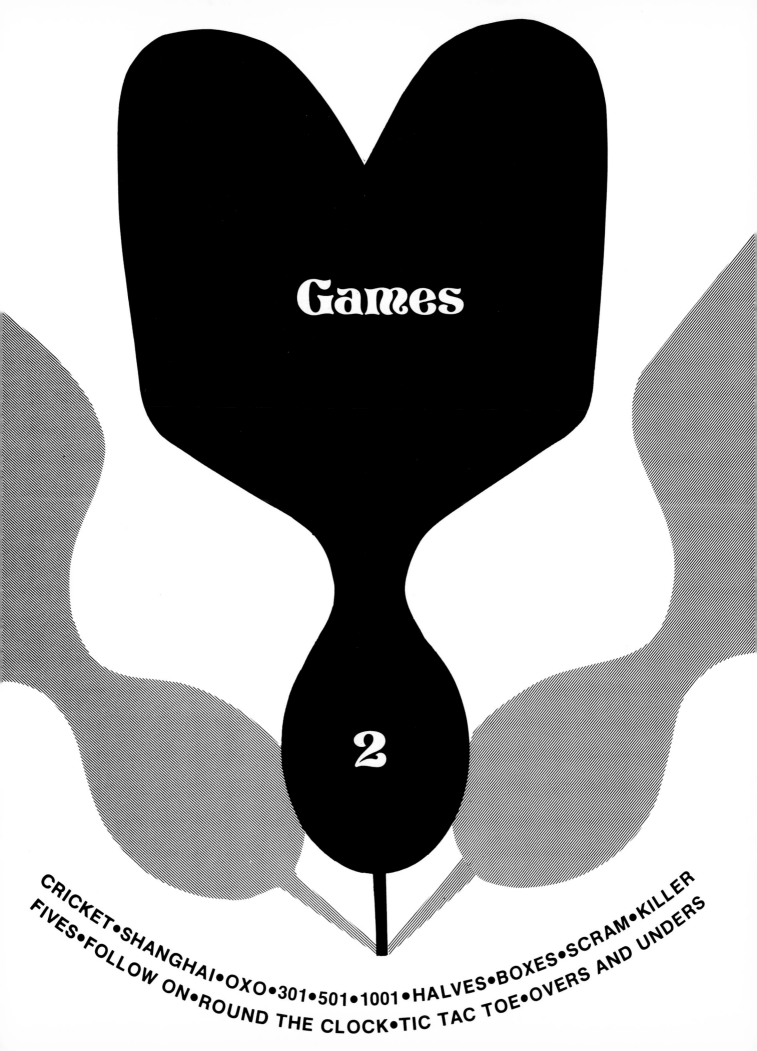

Games

2

CRICKET•SHANGHAI•OXO•301•501•1001•HALVES•BOXES•SCRAM•KILLER
FIVES•FOLLOW ON•ROUND THE CLOCK•TIC TAC TOE•OVERS AND UNDERS

Like most games, darts grew up in a casual and unregulated way. Thus, especially in England, rules vary in subtle ways between one area and another. So also do the names of the various games, not only between English regions but between England and America. This is, of course, part of the fascination with the lore of the game. It also means that it is proper etiquette for the visitor to play the "house rules." However, with increased competitive play at the national and international level, the basic games have become more standardized. In the descriptions that follow we have tried to give what seem to be the most generally agreed rules while making note of variations where these seem useful. We have also described a number of secondary games that may not be generally known within the American darts community. These games, while not used in competition, provide interesting variations, useful forms of practice, and in some cases a greater opportunity for the novice to match up to the expert.

301

This is the classic English game. The object of the game is to score 301 points exactly. Each player starts with 301 and aims to reduce it to zero. To decide who throws first, the players may toss a coin or throw one dart each at the bull, the nearest to the bull throwing first. A throw, as in all darts games, consists of three darts, players throwing alternately. Before a player can start scoring, he must first throw a dart in the double ring. Once he has thrown a double, that double and the scores that follow all count. Thus, if he scores a double 20 followed by a single 20 and a treble 5, he would deduct 75 from 301, so that the scoreboard would look like this:

	Sam	Don
	301	301
75	226	

As has been noted, each player must score 301 exactly; but the final dart to achieve this must, like the opening dart, be a double. Thus if a player is left with 40, he can win by throwing a double 20 (often marked on the scoreboard by x20), but not by throwing two single 20s. This means that a player in the course of a game must aim to get on an even number. For example, a player left with 51 could throw a single 11 leaving x20 or a single 19 leaving x16. He could also, although it is an unlikely strategy, throw 1 and a bull, as the bull represents double 25. If in the course of one throw a player goes over the required number, he is said to be "bust" and his score reverts to what it was at the end of the previous throw. For example, a player left with a total of 8 is on x4. In his first throw he gets a single 4 leaving x2. In his second throw he gets a single 17. His throw is then over and his score reverts to x4.

A complete game might score like this:

	Sam	Don	
	301	301	
60	241	275	26
100	141	234	41
45	96	177	57
45	51	144	33
19	x16	84	60

We will assume that Sam won the game by getting his x16 or a single 16 followed by x8, or some other combination.

The game of "301" is frequently played in three "legs," or the best out of three games. If after the first two "legs" the players stand one game each, then it is usual to throw for a bull or toss a coin to decide who throws first in the final game.

Variations

In a doubles game each of the players takes alternate throws and usually only one player on each side is required to get the opening double. Sometimes in a game the target is raised to 501 with an open start, i.e., no opening double required. This is the rule in the British *News of the World* Championship and the U.S. Open. In team games of, say, seven players a side, the target becomes 1001, again with an open start.

In some places a "no-bust" rule applies. In this case a player aiming at x4 getting a single 4 and then aiming at a x2 and getting a single 15 would leave a target of x2 and not revert to x4. In addition to these major variations, there are other local or house rules. For example, it is sometimes accepted that "three in a bed" (three darts in the same treble or double) wins the game. Another example: a player left with a single 1 may be allowed to throw for a double ½, represented by the space between the legs of the number 11; this is called "splitting eleven." Such variations have no competitive status and are always subject to prior agreement among the players.

Strategy

The Opening Double. Top-class players have an "all round the board" ability and may aim to go for a high double such as x20. The average player might be advised to go for one of the side doubles, say x13 or x14. The reason for this is that of the two basic factors determining an accurate darts throw—direction and strength—it is the latter that is the more difficult to judge. This is somewhat similar to putting in golf. It is not difficult to line up the club with the ball and the hole and, if strength were of no account, to bang the ball reasonably straight. It is, however, lack of certainty about strength that can produce the wrongly directed stroke. Thus a dart flung at x20 may be well within the broad vertical limits of the number but fall above or below the narrower horizontal limits. On the other hand, a dart flung at x13 may, if thrown too strongly, get into x4 or, if too softly, fall into x6.

Scoring. As we have noted, the highest number on the board is 60 (treble 20), and good players will be aiming at that number or at treble 19, if they happen to favor the bottom of the board. It will be noted, however, that the anonymous fiend who designed the board has cunningly placed high numbers next to low ones. Twenty is thus flanked by 5 and 1, and 19 by 7 and 3. The average player may well aim at 20 but end up by getting the familiar combination of 26 (20, 5, and 1) or worse. Clearly any player who wishes to play up to a reasonable standard should aim to be able to get two out of three of any number aimed at. For the beginner, however, it is worth noting that there are safe areas on the board, such as the 11-14-9 cluster. Darts thrown at the trebles of these numbers have a chance of a reasonable score or even quite a good one.

The Closing Double. Anyone aiming at a high standard of play must master the mathematics of the board. A good player will know almost immediately what he requires to score to get him on a particular double. Darts, indeed, might be a useful way of teaching elementary mathematics to young people. It is notable, however, that many darts players are able to make quick calculations in the course of play but are at a loss when faced with similar problems away from the board. Their ability is a practical one based on many years of play. Faced with a target of 114 they know, almost without thinking, that a treble 20 (60) leaves 54, which is all the 18s (i.e., single 18 and a game shot of a double 18). They have been in that situation before. A variety of charts suggesting ways of reaching the closing double have been produced by darts manufacturers and others. We reproduce our own versions of these charts in Chapter 5. However, some basic remarks about finishing a "301" game are in order now.

A number of conclusions can be drawn from the charts (see page 61). We should note first that the highest number at which a game can be finished in three darts is 170. This must be kept in mind as the score approaches this number and comes inside it. Faced with a three-figure number still to get, the impulse for the unthinking player is merely to continue to score high. For example, a player needing 113 shoots at the 20 and gets a single and is left with 93. He shoots again and gets a treble 20 (60), leaving him with the odd number 33. As the chart indicates, the proper strategy would have been 20, treble 19 (57), and double 18. Once within the range of a double, the player should work out his strategy while his opponent is playing, so that when he comes up to throw he knows what he has to achieve. The importance of being able to calculate quickly and reassess the situation (should the first dart not be lodged in the intended target) is in the need to maintain concentration and tempo. Nothing is more likely to break concentration than the need to do ponderous mental sums between each throw.

It is obvious that in most situations a number of choices are open. Faced with, say, 35 left, there are several doubles available. A 5 will leave double 15, a 15 double 10, and so on. The best choice, however, is 3 double 16. There are two reasons for this. At the bottom of the board there is a cluster of odd numbers from 7 to 17. A dart on any of these will leave the player with a double. In contrast, a dart aimed at 5 may well land in the 20 or 12, still leaving an odd number. Furthermore, the 5 leaves double 15 and a dart aimed at that double may well hit a single 15, returning the player once again to an odd number. In contrast, the 3 double 16 combination means that a single 16 leaves a double 8, a single 8 leaves a double 4, and a single 4 a double 2. It is because of this sequence of even numbers that double 16 is often referred to as the classic finishing double. The top-class player will, of course, aim to be efficient "all round the board," but it is worth keeping this pattern in mind. In the example given, a further subtlety is to be noted: a single 19 will leave 16 (x8), thus allowing the player to enter the even number sequence. Thus the correct strategy is not only to throw for a 3 but to throw for the middle to left of that sector, so that if 3 is missed 19 will be scored. In general, the player should drill himself to be sure that, in aiming at a double, if he misses he will hit the single bed of that number—assuming of course that it will leave him with another double.

Similar patterns are familiar. With 42 left, for example, 10 will give a x16 finish, but 6 is adjacent, giving a x18 finish, so that the dart should be aimed high on the 10 to make sure that if it misses the 10, it hits the 6 and not the 15. As has been noted, 54 is all the 18s, as 48 is all the 16s. Some players like these combinations, as the first dart aimed at the fat end of a singles wedge acts as a kind of guide and practice throw for the finishing double. Again, left with a double 17, it is wise to throw somewhat right within the target area in the chance that a miss will land in 2, leaving double 16. A close inspection of the board will reveal other patterns, and the player should make himself familiar with them.

The minimum of darts required to finish a game of "301," starting and finishing with a double, is six. In top-class play this is achieved more often than one might expect. Recent issues of the English magazine *Darts World* have recorded more than once the following elegant finish: double 16, three treble 20s, treble 19, double 16.

Cricket

This game is called "Tactics" in some areas. In England (where the rules are slightly different), it goes under a variety of names, including "Scrubbers" and "Coach and Horses." Exactly why it is called "Cricket" in America is not clear; furthermore, the appellation is somewhat confusing, as there is an English darts game called "Cricket" that is completely different.

Next to "301," "Cricket" is perhaps the most widely played game. Only the numbers 15 through 20 and bull are used. The object of the game is for each player on a team to score three of every number including three bulls, the center bull counting for two. When one side has three of a number it can then score on that number until the opposing team gets three darts in the same number. Once both sides have three of a number it is then closed to further scoring by either side. Doubles and trebles count, so that a treble 20 counts for three 20s and at once commands that number. It will be seen, therefore, that it is essentially a game for accurate throwing at trebles. As an example of scoring, let us assume that the first player for Team A throws a treble 20, a single 20, and a 5. That side will then command 20s and will have scored 20. Team B throws and scores a single 20, a double 20 (closing the 20s), and then a treble 19. Team A follows, throwing a single 19, a treble 19 (closing 19s but not scoring), and a single 18. The scoreboard will look like this:

	Team A	Team B
20	+/+ 20	+/+
19	+/+	+/+
18	/	
17		
16		
15		
0		

The vertical lines indicate the times a number has been hit and the horizontal line indicates that a number is closed. Team A has scored 20, having had four 20s before Team B had three.

The game finishes when all numbers have been closed, the team with the highest score winning.

It will be seen that the game offers the option of scoring or preventing opponents from scoring. Frequently players will go round the numbers in descending order, aiming to command them all. However, it may sometimes be good tactics to establish a score on a number once commanded. Assuming 20 and 19 are open, a heavy score on these numbers (rather than going on to 18) can put considerable pressure on the opposing team for the rest of the game. Again, in a case where a side has raced ahead to command 20 and 19 with these numbers still open, it may be good tactics for the opposing side not to plod after them but to throw for, say, 17 in the hope of commanding it and scoring rapidly. Two treble 17s can change the whole game and disorient the opposition.

Variations

A basic variation is in the rule concerning lucky darts. In most cases lucky darts are allowed to count. That is to say, a dart aimed at 20 but landing in 18 scores. In some areas, such as Boston (where the game is called "Tactics"), the player must call the number being aimed at and only darts in that number are allowed to count. Lucky darts are referred to by various names such as "fallout" or, in England, "dew drops."

In one English variant of the game, which we will refer to as "Coach and Horses," the numbers are extended to include 10 to 14. This makes a distinctive difference, as 11 and 14 are side by side, as are 15 and 10, thus offering a bigger target area. "Coach and Horses" is, therefore, a good team game for players of mixed ability, especially when each side is composed of a strong and a weak player. In such a case the strong player can concentrate on closing the higher numbers while his partner pounds away at the 11/14 and 10/15 trebles. An alternate strategy is for the weaker player to go at once for the bull with the chance of picking up a few "dew drops" on the way. This of course operates only if "fallout" is permitted.

Shanghai

In the original version of this game, of which there are a number of variants, each player takes it in turn to throw three darts at each segment in turn from 1 to 20 (or, if a shorter version is agreed upon, 1 to 10). Only darts landing in the segment aimed at count towards the score. Doubles and trebles count. Thus a player aiming at segment 4 and landing darts in single 4, treble 4, and single 18 scores a total of 16 for that throw. Obviously it is important in this game to throw well in the later stages, which involve the higher scoring numbers. "Shanghai" is the name given to scoring the single, double, and treble of the same number in one throw. The normal rule is that the last dart must be a double or a treble. A "Shanghai" scored during the game is game shot and wins the game outright.

The game can be played as singles or doubles (players on the same side throwing consecutively or almost any number of players playing as individuals).

Oxo

The same game as "Shanghai," but with two variations. The numbers to be aimed at are selected by the players throwing darts at the board with their non-throwing hand or by throwing three darts simultaneously. Scoring is also different inasmuch as only one point is scored per segment (two points for a double and three for a treble), regardless of the number. Thus a throw at number six consisting of two single sixes and a treble six scores only 5 and not 30.

Halves

This game, in our view the best of the various "Shanghai" games, is called "Shanghai" in some areas. Certain numbers are given: 20; a double (any double); a treble (any treble); a bull (inner bull counting for two, the outer for one, as is usual); and 41. This last number must be scored exactly in three darts, all darts counting, so that there is no score if one dart is flung off the board or bounces out of a wire. To these standard numbers are added others chosen at random or selected by the players. Let us suppose, for the sake of the example to be given, that the numbers 17, 13, 18, and 16 have been chosen. These are usually set out on the scoreboard starting with one of the single numbers and ending with the 20 and the bull. The players throw nearest the bull to see who will go last, it being an advantage in this game to throw last — knowing what you must get to beat the other players. Again, "Halves" can be played as a singles or team game. Each side starts with a score of 50. Players (or sides) take it in turn to throw at each selected number. As in "Shanghai," they can score only on that number. The crucial distinction is that the cumulative score is cut in half if, in any throw, none of the three darts hits the selected target.

Let us set out an example:

	Dick	(50)	*Charlie*
17	84		84
13	123		97
D	135		49
18	189		67
T	249		70
16	281		118
41	141		159
20	161		219
B	82		244

In the example given, it will be seen that both players threw two 17s each, which, added to 50, gave each of them a first score of 84. Dick then threw well, throwing three 13s, a double 6, three 18s, a treble 20, and two 16s. But then his game collapsed and he failed to get his 41 or a bull and only threw one 20. Charlie, who had fallen behind by scoring low and failing to get a double, had a strong finish, managing to get both 41 and an outer bull. The example shows that the state of this game can change rapidly. This is one of its competitive virtues and, in that sense, is suitable for players of mixed ability. Another advantage is that it has a fixed termination independent of the skill of the players and is, thus again, suitable for players of less than average ability.

Any player must, of course, learn how to play "301," but for the beginner the effort to get that opening double (to say nothing of the closing double) can be a long, painful, and embarrassing experience.

In "Halves," as in other versions of the game, a Shanghai is game shot.

Round the Clock

This is a suitable game for an uneven number of players, each player throwing for himself. In its simplest form (there are a number of variations), the players aim to go round the board from 1 to 20, scoring one of each number and ending on the bull, the first to finish winning the game.

Variations

In one form of the game, if a player's last dart lands in the required number he is allowed another throw. In this version, of course, it is possible for a player to complete the game before others have thrown. To avoid this, each player is allowed the same number of throws. In another version the double ring is brought into play. Thus, if a player aiming at the 2 segment scores a double 2 (4), he is then allowed to proceed to 5. The last number at which this applies is obviously 10.

"Round the Board" is also a good practice game, and expert players can improve their game by going round the board in doubles and trebles.

Killer

Again, this is a game that can be played by an uneven number of players.

To start, each player throws a wrong-handed dart at the board to select a double. Thus, a player landing a dart in 7 is on double 7. The first stage is for each player to get a dart on his own double. Once he does this he becomes a Killer and can now aim his darts at his opponents' doubles. Each player has three "lives" and loses one each time a dart (including his own, by mistake) hits his double. The player left with one or more lives is the winner. The game is much loved by highly competitive, not to say aggressive, players. It can lead to a good deal of bargaining among the group, players ganging up on another who is forging ahead, on the assumed best player, or even on a player not especially popular. "Killer" is a game leading either to much good-natured banter or to abuse and invective, according to temperament.

Scram

This is a simple game for two players, one called the Stopper and the other the Scorer.

The Stopper throws first by aiming to get a dart into each of the highest numbers (it is a matter of choice as to whether 25 and 50 are included). Any number hit by one of the Stopper's darts is not available for the Scorer, who must throw at numbers not commanded by the Stopper. This first leg continues until all numbers are ruled out. The roles are then reversed, the player with the highest score at the end of both legs being the winner.

Follow On

Once more, this is a game for an uneven-sized group and probably best played that way.

The basis of the game is that each player must get a dart into whatever number was left by the previous player. Thus if a player leaves a 25, the next player must get a 25 in two darts and then aim to leave something equally difficult for the player to follow. Each player has three lives; should he fail to get the required number in one throw of three darts, he loses a life. The next player must attempt to get that same number. For this game it is usual for the single segment to be divided into two, the inner single (between the treble ring and the 25) and the outer single (between the treble ring and the double ring). In some bizarre versions, other segments are created, such as the 0 in the number 20 or the triangle of number 4, but this is best left to eccentrics. The first dart flung by the player starting the game to land on the scoring area becomes the target for the next player. As it is important to leave a difficult target, he may aim his first two darts at the double ring, trying to make sure that if he does not get a double he will land outside the scoring area. Should he fail to get a double but not score, he must be sure to score on his third dart, otherwise he will lose a life, in which case he will probably aim at the bull on the assumption that if he does not get a 50 or 25 he will at least get an inner single. The player with one or more lives left at the end of the game is the winner. This is a relaxed and diverting group game that also calls for accurate throwing.

Boxes

This is a simple game, but useful practice for high scoring. Best played as a singles game, it can also be played as doubles or with an uneven group. The player throwing first aims to score as high as possible. The next player must equal or beat that score or have his number boxed. Whatever number he leaves must be equaled or beaten by his opponent. A player having three or five boxes (the number agreed on beforehand) loses.

Example: Score

Luis	Gene
120	80
85	100
22	33
140	100
70	60

The main option in the game is whether merely to aim at beating the number or to set a high target. In the example above, Luis left a 22 (probably a 20 followed by two 1s) and Gene played safe by going for the left-hand side trebles but only scored three single 11s.

Overs and Unders

This game is a simple variation of "Boxes" in which a second leg is added by having as a target the lowest score. An amusing diversion, as it is surprising how often among reasonably good players a high score is achieved in aiming at a low one. In aiming at three single 1s, it is remarkable how difficult it is to prevent a dart from lodging in treble 20 or treble 18.

Fives

Again this is a game open to any number of players. The object is to achieve in one throw a number divisible by 5. Each multiple of 5 scores a point. Thus 120 scores 24, 40 scores 8, and so on. The final target is to score 51 exactly. Thus a player with a total of 44 requires 7, so must shoot 35 (7 x 5). A score over 51 is bust and the player reverts to his previous score.

This game is for those who can calculate reasonably well, otherwise more time is spent dividing than throwing. It will be clear that certain target areas, namely the 20/5 and 10/15 combinations, come much into play.

Tic Tac Toe

This is based on the familiar pencil-and-paper game called "Noughts and Crosses" in England. The bull is used, plus eight numbers chosen in whatever fashion the players decide. An example would be as follows:

17	16	4
19	50	11
5	15	20

The game can be played with single numbers but is best played demanding doubles or trebles. The object, as in the original game, is to command a vertical, horizontal, or diagonal line. The advantage to a player in scoring a bull first is obvious.

The Basics

A discussion of the "technique" of darts throwing may at first seem ludicrous. After all, the game is so overtly simple: one simply hurls the dart at the dart board. There need be little attention paid to form, rhythm, tempo, or the other elements of "technique" commonly associated with more complex and difficult sports such as golf or tennis. If one hurls the dart often enough (i.e., practices) then one becomes quite accurate in terms of where it will land. After much practice a greater percentage of the darts will land in the target area rather than in the wall. It is sadly true that this description quite accurately fits the average home dart bomber—the cork board basement artist whose favorite and only game is "Bulls."

However, for the serious player, or for anyone who aspires to be a serious player, considerations of technique are extremely important. We argue—and our argument can be verified by an examination of the styles of the finest players of the game—that the dart throw involves a *stroke,* a stroke that is as important to the accuracy of pegging a double 16 as a smooth rhythmic putting stroke in golf is to sinking a 16-footer. The analogy between these two sports is appropriate, particularly if in relating to golf one considers putting as opposed to the swing with woods and irons. In the dart throw, as in putting, various elements—such as stance, grip, and weight distribution—can vary greatly from player to player, even among the finest players in the world. Yet within this variety there are certain basic similarities. In this chapter we shall discuss the various approaches to dart throwing and will attempt to isolate and analyze those elements of all styles that are fundamental and necessary to good darting.

Stance

The first and most obvious consideration of darts technique is the stance, or the position of the feet and the balance of the body at the hockey line. It is in the stance that one finds the greatest variety among dart throwers. There are essentially three basic approaches: the head-on stance, with both feet and body facing the board; the three-quarters stance, with the feet and body angled to the board; and the sideways stance, with the feet and body at a ninety-degree angle to the board for shooting.

The one stance that is virtually never used by good players is the "pitcher" stance. When employing this stance, the throwing arm and shoulder are angled away from the board rather than toward it (as in the other stances mentioned). To throw from this type of position results in a baseball type of throw. It is interesting that most players first adopt this stance when first learning the game—it seems the most natural for throwing. As will be discussed later in this chapter, this throw forces shoulder movement and body pivot and is therefore inadvisable.

There are limitless variations in stance used by players. These are all based on the three basic types discussed above.

There is no proper or ideal stance among all these variations. Virtually all are used by fine players of the game. It is our observation that the full-front stance and variations of it are more common among English darters, while the three-quarters and sideways stances are more prevalent in America.

Regardless of the particular stance employed, there are several fun-

The Stance

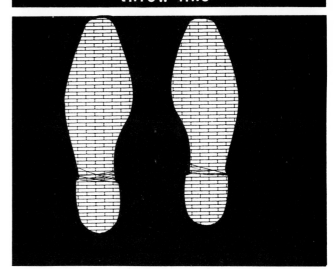

1

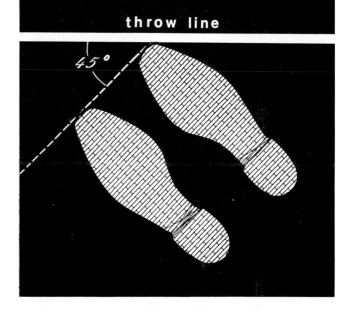

2

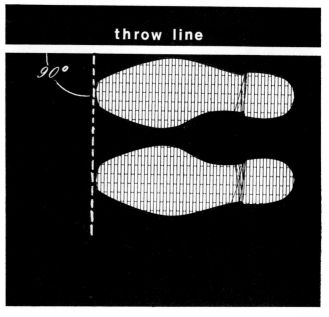

3

damentals of weight distribution and body position that are important to accurate throwing. First, the weight should be distributed evenly, or almost evenly, on both feet. Some players, using a sideways or three-quarters stance, lean over the forward foot and put sixty to seventy percent of the body weight over this foot.

While this can be an effective shooting position, it can also create problems for the beginner. The basic principle in weight distribution is to position and distribute the weight as comfortably as possible while at the same time striving to eliminate any body movement during the throw. With the weight distributed evenly, body sway or movement can be minimized. When a greater percentage of the weight is over the forward foot, there is a tendency to rock or sway over this foot during the throw. Good players who use a three-quarters or sideways stance and who do "lean" have usually mastered this tendency and can effectively lean out over the forward foot without moving the body during the throw. This consideration of body sway or movement is a vital element of darting technique. Any body movement will affect the flight of the dart. So to eliminate body movement is to lessen the number of variables that can affect the flight of the dart. Thus the thrower is freer to concentrate on fewer variables in order to perfect accuracy.

Although we are discussing these fundamentals as hard and fast rules, we wish to make it clear, indeed, that they are not. There are many fine players who rock and sway with each throw. However, they are the exception, and their skills are the result of a great deal of practice resulting in a "groove" — an unorthodox throw that through practice becomes very accurate. The great majority of good darters follow the fundamentals of eliminating body movement during the throw.

Grip

The second element of darts technique is the grip. Here, too, there is a great deal of variation among players. Essentially there are three types of grip: the thumb and two-finger, the thumb and three-finger, and the thumb and four-finger grips.

Most beginning players start with the thumb and two-finger grip, as this is initially the most natural and comfortable. In this grip the thumb is positioned under the balance point of the dart with the forefinger and middle finger gripping the barrel of the dart. This grip is the simplest and should therefore be the first grip tried. With only two fingers gripping the barrel of the dart, there is less chance of a stray pinkie affecting the flight of the dart as it is released.

For more pinpoint accuracy, many players adopt the three- or four-finger grip. In these grips the third and perhaps the fourth finger are extended over the pointed shaft. This grip can create greater accuracy for the player who has begun to develop a fine stroke using the two-finger grip. However, in this more complex grip, there is a tendency to "steer" the dart toward the target. And while trying to "steer," a player can often develop a hitch in the throwing style, which makes the darts less accurate.

Some players change the grip slightly in order to shoot more accurately at certain areas of the board. For example, in shooting at a double 16 or double 8, one might move the thumb and fingers slightly forward in an effort to

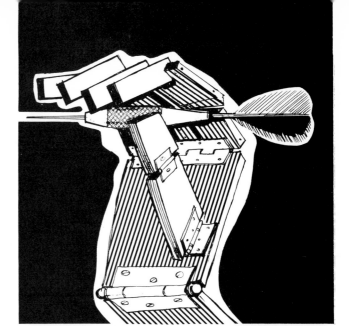

two-finger

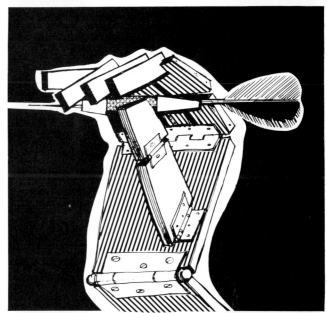

three-finger

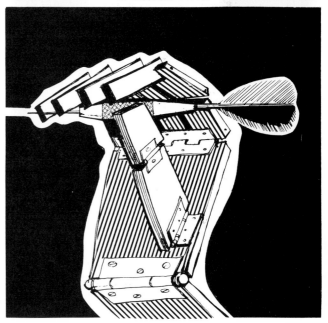

four-finger

"bloop" the dart into the double. For a double 20 or double 1, the fingers and thumb might be moved slightly back on the barrel in order to propel the dart into one of these high doubles. Some very fine players actually change the grip slightly to shoot over an existing dart in the board. Thus, in shooting at 20s, if the first dart lands just low of the treble 20, the fingers and thumb might be moved back a fraction on the barrel in order to peg the second dart above the existing dart and into the treble 20.

It is our suggestion that one begin with the two-finger grip and after a time experiment with more complex grips for shooting at different areas on the board. Of course all experimentation should take place while practicing, never in the heat of a match.

Stroke

The third and final basic element of darts technique is something we shall call elbow-wrist-fingertip coordination, or, if you will, simply *stroke*. The stroke of the darts throw is determined by the interaction of the elbow, wrist, and fingertips. It is in the stroke that one finds the greatest similarity among all good darts throwers.

Probably the sport most similar to darts (in terms of stroke) is pool. The pool stroke is also dependent on the interaction of the elbow, wrist, and fingertips. Thus in a pool stroke the thumb and fingertips grip the pool cue, and the wrist and elbow combine to create a smooth, rhythmic pendulum motion—which results in a stroke.

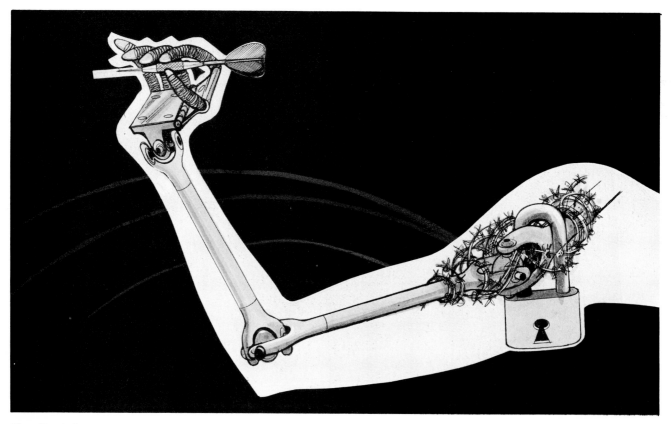

The Pool Stroke

In dart throwing the pendulum motion is reversed—the forearm points upwards rather than downwards, but the basic motion is essentially the same. The elbow provides the initial pendulum movement; nearing the point of release, the wrist moves forward slightly and the fingertips and thumb open forward towards the target.

To isolate these various functions: the elbow motion starts the throw, and for every throw to any area on the board the elbow motion should be essentially the same in rhythm and tempo. The wrist and fingers interacting determine the release point of the dart and therefore determine also the vertical on the board at which the dart will land. An early release will result in a dart landing high on the board and a later release will cause a dart to land low on the board.

As in a great many sports involving a stroke, the key to a good dart throw is tempo and rhythm. The main ingredients of the stroke should be the same for every throw, the only variation being the point of release. Therefore, the pendulum motion of the elbow should be smooth and fluid from the start of the throw (the backswing) through the release point and follow-through. The stroke, then, determines the vertical path of the dart. A player with a smooth stroke can shoot a dart into any vertical by simply angling his arm and head in the direction of the desired vertical. Some players prefer to move along the hockey line in order to establish the desired vertical path. Others simply angle the head and arm toward the path. The former method has merit in that it actually lessens the distance the dart must travel to the target area.

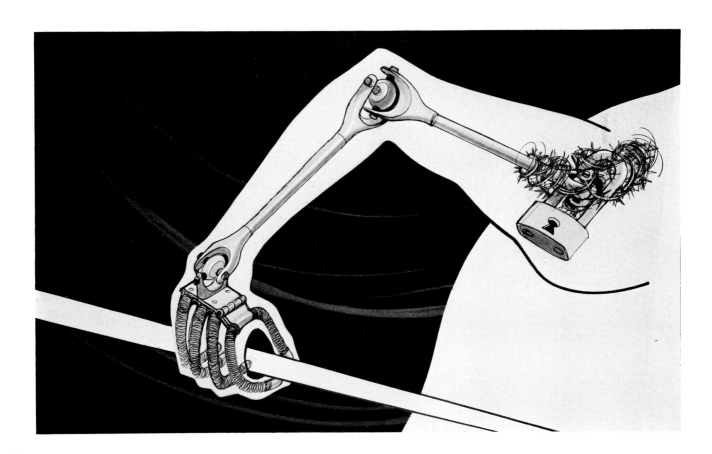

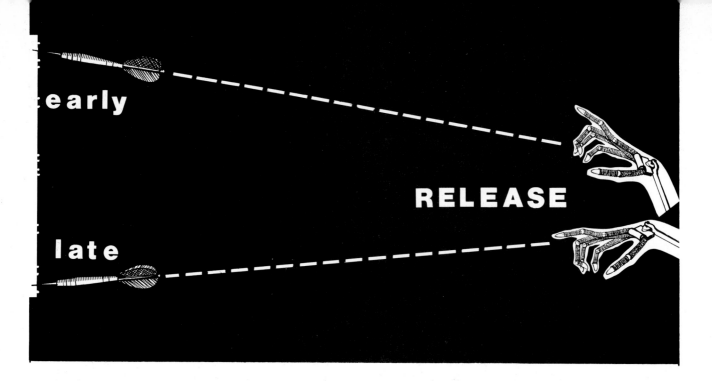

Thus, shifting the feet and body several inches to the left of center of the hockey line can make shooting at a left-side double (double 8 or double 16, for example) a little easier. In moving along the hockey line in this fashion, a player can maintain the same stroke, the same angling of head, shoulder, and feet, and the same distance from dart to target for every shot. As the actual playing area on the board is only 13¼" it would seem to make little sense to move more than 6–7" to the left or right of the center of the line to improve one's shot at an outside double. Most players who practice this method rarely move more than 6" off of center.

Occasionally it might be necessary to move along the line in order to shoot around a dart that is blocking off a given target area. Thus if the first dart thrown lands squarely in the middle of the treble 20, a player might move to the left or right several inches in order to shoot the next dart into the same treble. Similarly, in shooting for a double 16, if the first two darts land just outside the double on the wire and thereby create an obstruction to the double, a player might move several inches to the right in order to gain a more clear and distinct shot at the target. This practice does create an unobstructed flight path to the target, but at the same time it makes the distance to the target greater.

Some players, while attempting to demonstrate a little flair, carry this method to extremes. Thus, after throwing the first dart into the center of the treble 20, the above-mentioned player will move as much as two or three feet to the left or right of the center of the hockey line for the second shot. Although this practice may look very impressive to the uninformed observer, in fact it makes little sense at all. A two- or three-foot shift off of center will substantially increase the actual throwing distance from dart to target and therefore make the shot more difficult, rather than easier.

In summary, shifting position along the hockey line can be a useful technique for certain types of shots, and many excellent players use this technique to great advantage. However, in most instances the shift should be only a few inches one way or the other, as to move a greater distance will usually make the throw more difficult because of the resulting greater dart-to-target distance.

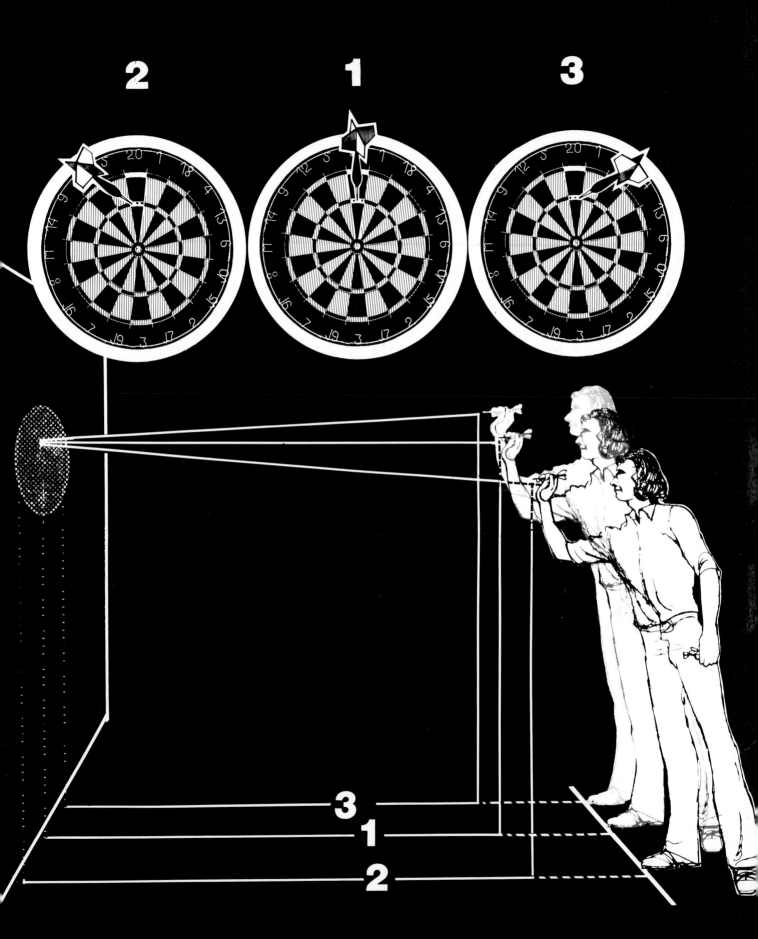

Moving Along the Hockey

Speed

The speed of the throw, and the resulting speed of the propelled dart, are the next consideration. Speed directly affects the arc of the dart during flight. Slower speed will necessarily result in a high arc, or "bloop," as it is sometimes called. A faster speed will decrease the arc and make the dart travel in a straighter line of flight. There seems to be no standard among good players as to speed. There are many fine players who bloop every dart at the target; there are also many excellent throwers who hurl their darts with a great deal of speed, the arrows having virtually no arc at all. It is our recommendation that for beginners a medium or slow speed be used at first. The dart should have a slight arc in its path to the target. This speed is best for developing and perfecting a rhythmic stroke. After much practice—and the resulting elevation in confidence—one can begin to experiment with faster and slower speeds. Initial experimentation with faster speeds will usually result in less accuracy. The darts will seem to fly truer and straighter, but the acceleration in the elbow movement necessary for greater speed can often create a slight hitch in the stroke, resulting in considerably less accuracy, both vertical and horizontal. If the fluid motion of the stroke can be maintained while throwing harder, then additional speed has several advantages. First, a faster dart will bounce out of the board or off of a wire less often than a slower dart. Second, the faster dart tends to enter the board at a more perfect angle (90° to the board surface) than a slower dart.

The faster dart will therefore create less of an obstruction to other darts thrown to the same area. The blooped dart can often block off a given target area because of the angle of the dart in the board. Of course the weight of the dart, the length of the shaft, and the design of the flight also contribute to the angle of entry (see Chapter 4).

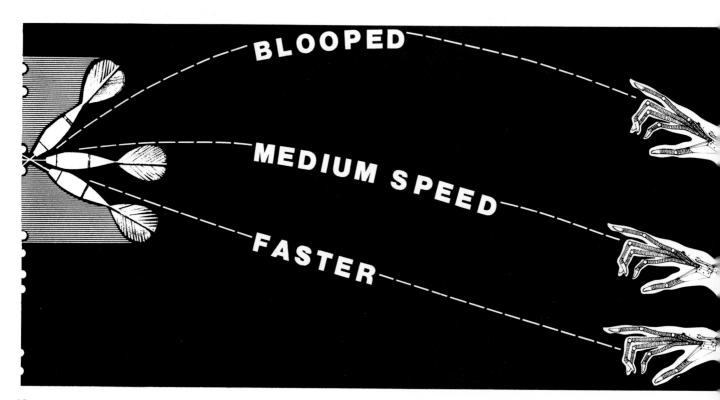

Trouble-Shooting

Even very fine players make poor throws on occasion. A brief scenario will serve as an example of this:

In a tense match—his fingertips damp with perspiration, his vision blurred slightly by untold pints and heavy smoke filling the bar—Bud B., a fine pub player, steps to the hockey line needing a double 16 to close. His opponent is on double 8 and the last three arrows were right on the wire. Bud steps forward, wipes his right hand several times on the seat of his trousers, and stares at his target for ten seconds, summoning up his concentration. He takes his stance and throws—a single 11. Disaster. He must now shoot a 5 and a double 8 in two darts if he hopes to win, which of course he does.

What went wrong with the first throw? The skill was there—Bud is a practiced competitive player with a fine smooth stroke. The concentration was there—Bud took his time at the hockey line and concentrated on his target and on how to get it. But the dart still landed way off target. In all likelihood the poor throw resulted from some tiny error at the point of Bud's release. The stroke was probably smooth and good, but at the height of the throw Bud released early and the dart floated high into the 11. This poor release may have been caused by the tension of the game. The baseball term "wild and high," used to describe a pitcher who while under pressure releases the ball early and therefore throws high into the strike zone or out of it, has relevance to dart throwing. In the pressure of a match, the release point is most often affected and the result is a throw that is high or low in relation to the target.

A dart that is wild horizontally can often be the result of an error in the fingertip and thumb release. A slight flick or twist in the fingertip or thumb can propel a dart wildly off vertical and into disastrous sections of the board.

The secret to overcoming these problems is not simple. If it were, we would be taking cash prizes at the *News of the World* Championship and the North American Open instead of writing books. Be that as it may, practice and a great deal of it is essential, of course. But first and foremost is concentration. At the hockey line one must strain to think about all the elements of the forthcoming shot and eliminate from thought all extraneous factors. Jack Nicklaus could serve as a model to any darter. As Nicklaus prepares to putt, he is focusing all his mental energy on making the putt and, importantly, he has a great deal of confidence in his ability to do so. Therefore, in your next approach to the hockey line for a double 16 game shot, try the following:

1. Think about the dart you will be throwing.

2. Make a mental picture of your stroke and the path of the dart to the target.

3. Stare at the target and only the target (in all probability it will become larger).

4. While still staring and concentrating, take your stance comfortably.

5. Pause.

6. Think to yourself, "I cannot miss; there is no way this arrow can stay out of the double 16."

7. Marvel at the enormousness of the target.
8. Throw smoothly and confidently.
9. Now do the same for your next two shots: 5, double 8.

We cannot overemphasize the importance of concentration in good darting. It is often, perhaps always, the ability to concentrate on every shot that separates the good or excellent player from the average one. Some examples of players at a local pub will serve further to illustrate this point.

Howard is one of the best players in the pub. He has a very smooth stroke, a light touch. He shoots for good score and on closing doubles Howard is unbeatable. He doesn't take a long time concentrating at the hockey line, but when he throws he is obviously ready mentally. For example, Howard approaches the line with 74 remaining (playing "301"). He concentrates and throws a single 14 (shooting for a neat finish: treble 14, double 16 = 74). Unflustered, Howard changes position slightly and then throws a single 20, double 20 game shot. Obviously Howard was thinking and concentrating during his entire turn. He had decided on a strategy (treble 14, double 16) to close, but was also prepared to miss on any given shot and change strategy without losing his concentration at the line.

In practice Buster looks like the best player in the city. He can regularly throw a ton (100) or ton-forty (140), and all his practice darts are right around the treble (T20). However, Buster is everyone's favorite opponent. In the course of an evening he spends as much time making trips to the bar buying drinks for winning opponents as he does actually throwing darts. And, ironically, Buster seems to concentrate at the line as much or more than anybody. But does he really concentrate? What follows may reveal the problem. Buster steps to the line needing 52 to finish: an ideal close in "301"—20, double 16. He stands at the line for 15-20 seconds staring at his target. He throws a single 1—not a very good shot, but one that can happen to even the best of players. Very flustered, Buster grimaces, turns his back to the board, and tries to figure out what went wrong. He looks to the board again and while preparing to shoot must ask his partner, Roger, what he needs to finish. Roger hasn't been paying attention, so the two must go through the score: 52-1 = 51. After some deliberation they decide that 19, double 16 should be Buster's shot. He again concentrates for a considerable period of time and throws—a treble 7, again not a good shot. Buster goes through the same routine. After some deliberation he again approaches the line trying for a double 15 game shot. Now Buster really strains to concentrate on his target. He takes a full 30 seconds getting ready. He throws—a single 15.

In comparing the shooting and approaches to shooting of Howard and Buster we can begin to isolate a key element of successful darting. During his three darts Howard never once broke concentration. He had a planned "ideal" strategy and alternative strategies for missed shots. He threw smoothly, rhythmically, and with confidence. Poor Buster did none of this. He became flustered with a miss and had to resummon his concentration for every dart he was to throw. In the process he had no alternative strategies and with each miss had to recount and rethink the next throw. And we suspect that Buster's elaborate "concentration" actually consisted of his trying not to worry about the consequences of a bad shot, rather than pinpointing his mental energy on the winning shot.

A Note on Drink

Unlike most competitive sports, darts incorporates the consumption of alcoholic beverages as an important part of playing the game. This is quite natural, given that the game originated in English pubs. There is a discussion of the social role of drink and the game in the last chapter of this book.

Our concern here is the relationship of drink to techniques and concentration—or how drinking affects one's play. We are not social scientists, nor have we made any controlled studies in this area, but it is reasonably safe to say that there is considerable evidence to indicate that the consumption of alcoholic beverages affects reflexes, coordination, vision, and clear thinking. Therefore, drinking is rarely an activity associated with competitive sports. However, drinking is a common and important activity in pub darts play. Although money is occasionally wagered on a match, the stakes are most often a draught or pint. And of course, the winning stakes are invariably consumed during the next match.

Now, how does one drink, and play for drink, while continuing to throw competitive darts throughout the evening? We might simply answer, "Learn to hold your liquor," but this is evading the issue rather than coming to terms with it. There are several important points to be made here. First, it is our firm belief that a certain quantity of drink is necessary as a kind of lubricant to throw competitive darts. The "certain amount" depends, of course, upon the individual. The argument here is that a few beers (three to five, let's say) will actually improve one's throwing. The alcohol relaxes the nerves, loosens the joints, and gives one the ability to focus mental energy sharply (or at least think that mental energy is being sharply focused—and this may be just as important). Thus, the stroke becomes smoother and more fluid; the ability to concentrate is enhanced. And, importantly, one gains a great deal of confidence. So far, so good. These are the definite advantages to drinking while competing at darts—again, of course, relative to the individual's drinking experience and capacity.

Some players have the ability to drink steadily all through the evening and continue to throw winning darts. Others are less fortunate. Excess consumption of alcohol can have an extremely adverse effect on many a player. The first sign of this excess is a slight wildness accompanied by aggression and elevation of confidence. Initially the tipsy darter might be able to remain competitive with an occasional brilliant shot (brought about by enormous concentration), but eventually the drink will ruin his game. And unfortunately the steadily deteriorating reflexes and eye-hand coordination are complemented only by extreme confidence, determination, and the desire and conviction to win. The end result is usually terribly sloppy darts and a significant loss of money. Therefore, the intelligent player should know how much to drink, and most importantly, when to stop, either drinking or throwing—whichever seems most appropriate at the time.

Tools of the Trade

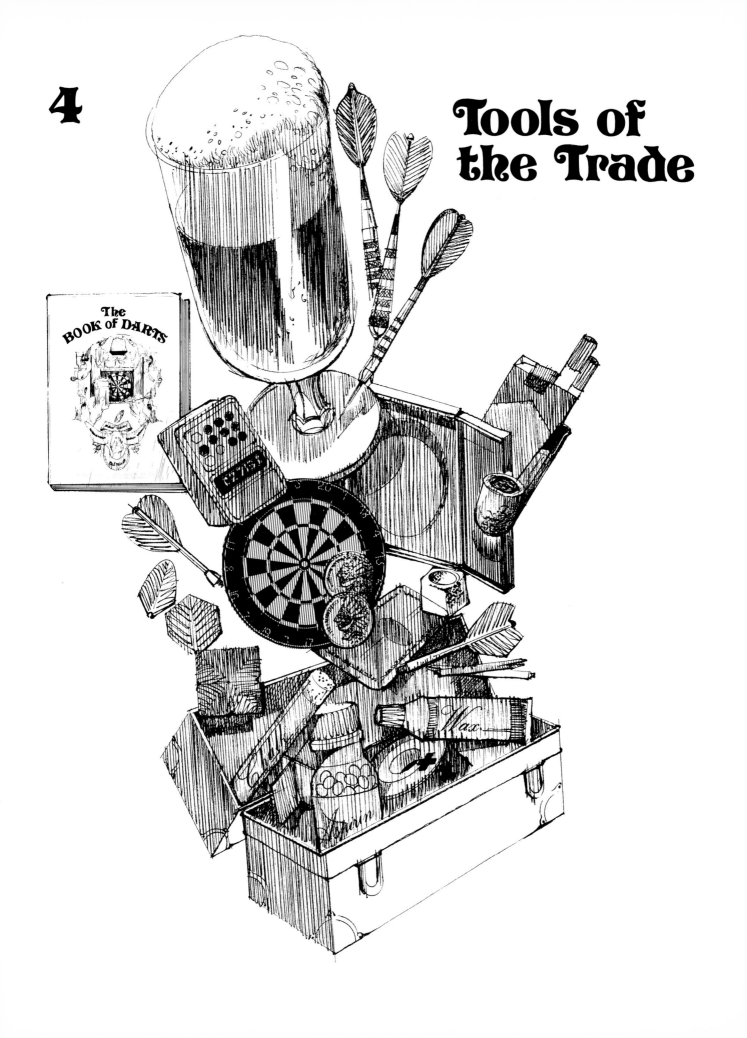

In this chapter the various tools and accessories used in darts playing will be discussed. The dart board and darts will be examined thoroughly as to types, models, brands, and prices. The final portion of this chapter will consist of a discussion and description of various darting accessories currently available.

The Board

All references to dart boards made under this heading are to the standard "clock" board as described in Chapter 1. The standard board is available in four different materials. These are cork, coiled paper, bristle, and elm.

Cork and coiled paper boards are the least expensive dart boards available on the market. Depending on thickness and wire design, these boards can be purchased for prices ranging from $5 to $15. Both these types of boards are available with welded or stapled metal wires, plastic instead of wire dividers, and wire numbers or painted numbers. Because of its relatively low cost, the paper or cork board is usually the first choice for a home board for the beginning dart player. However, both paper and cork boards have relatively short life spans when compared with bristle and elm boards. A dart, when striking one of these cheaper boards, leaves a permanent hole. Although for a time the board may self-seal the dart impression, after continued use dart holes begin appearing—darts striking these holes tend to bounce out. Furthermore, most of the inexpensive boards are usually only 5/8" to 1" thick and after a certain amount of use the board will warp. When this happens, the wires become unstapled from the surface of the board and, while the end result of a truly warped board with wildly protruding wires may be visually interesting, it is certainly not very useful for darts playing.

The standard board used in England and America is the bristle board, sometimes called the English bristle board. There are two major manufacturers of this type of board, Nodor and Winmau, and boards by these two companies are virtually identical. The bristle board is manufactured by packing a fiber material similar to rope fiber under great pressure. The bristle board consists of some 16 million fibers (or bristles) packed under 10 tons of pressure. The packed fibers are mounted against a wooden back frame to create the 1½" thickness of the board. The packed fibers are dyed with nonfading colors, which last the life of the board. The boards are hand-wired with high-tensile steel. The wire numbers are supported on a movable outer wire ring so that the board can be rotated as it begins to show wear in certain areas, and the numbers can be rotated via the movable outer ring to their proper positions. It is therefore recommended that one rotate a bristle board two spaces clockwise periodically (depending on use) to keep the 20s area from developing too much wear. The area around the treble 20 will usually be the first area on the board to fluff up—the bristles in this area will begin to bulge out and appear fluffy. In fact, the board should be turned before this begins to happen. Because the bullseye remains in the same place even though the board is rotated, it is usually the first area of the board to show significant wear. However, even though the bull may bulge out and soften up slightly, it will retain its ability to cushion darts for an indefinite period of time.

In pubs the most common reason for discarding bristle boards is wire damage, not a loss of cushioning in the surface of the board itself. After continued use the wires will bend and spread out of place in all numeral sections and in time there is no fresh wire area to which to turn the board.

Bristle boards are available in America for between $30 and $40, depending on specific design and retailer. A slightly more expensive bristle board is available with inlaid circular steel strips instead of the conventional wire rings. These steel strips last longer than wires; furthermore, because the strips are thinner they create larger treble, double, and bull target areas.

The elm board, which is a handmade log-end board, is rarely seen in America and is now used primarily in England for the *News of the World* Championship and in some pubs. This beautiful board has the finest cushioning of all dart boards and the finest wire construction. However, the elm board demands constant care. It must be soaked regularly so that it doesn't dry out and crack. Also, these boards can be easily and irreparably damaged by blunt, heavy darts.

Bristle boards, then, are the standard in the darts world. They can be found in virtually every darts bar in America, in most pubs in England, and on the walls in the homes of serious dart throwers everywhere. For the aspiring shooter the bristle board is an excellent lifetime investment and a virtual must for competitive darts play and practice.

Darts

At the time this book is being written, there are literally scores of companies around the world manufacturing darts of all types. The recent popularity of darts in America has been accompanied by the rise of a myriad of small companies manufacturing darts and darting accessories both in America and in England.

One could perhaps say that the modern form of marketing darts began in 1936 when Mr. Frank Lowy, a Hungarian immigrant living in London, had the idea to market three brass darts in a single package. Before this time darts had been sold individually. Mr. Lowy's first dart, the Silver Comet, became enormously successful when marketed in a package of three and has had a profound influence on the success and popularity of darts in the world. Mr. Lowy's enterprise was later to become Unicorn Products of London, which to this day is the largest manufacturer of darts and darts accessories in the world.

The modern dart can be classified according to shape, weight, length, type of flight, type of shaft, and type of material. A recent Unicorn darts catalog lists over 170 different darts barrels and weights alone. It is therefore safe to say that, given all the dart manufacturers in the world and all the models they market, there are truly thousands of designs of darts with varying weights, shafts, and flights available to the contemporary dart thrower. Of these thousands we will offer little advice as to which models are preferable. To do so would be impossible, as every dart thrower has a slightly different approach in attempting to hurl the arrow into the mythical treble 20, and therefore has different needs as to weight, shape, etc.

Of all the types of darts on the market, there are three basic barrel shapes. These are (1) darts with the weight distributed evenly throughout the length of the barrel; (2) darts with the weight concentrated in the middle of the barrel; (3) darts with the weight concentrated forward on the barrel:

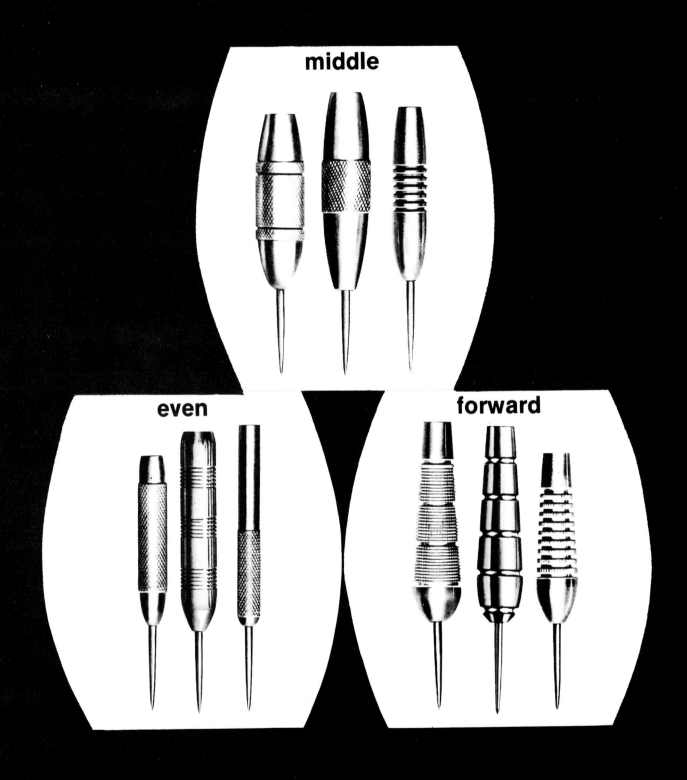

middle

even

forward

Barrel Shapes

Given the same weight, flight design, throwing motion, and speed, these three basic barrel shapes will fly and strike the board in different ways. The barrel with even weight distribution will tend to fly level and strike the board at close to a 90° angle. The barrel with middle weight concentration will tend to fly with the point heading upward and will strike the board similarly. The torpedo-designed dart, with the weight concentrated forward, will fly with the tip angling downward and will strike the board at a similar angle.

These descriptions of flight and striking patterns are in fact only generalizations and cannot be separated from considerations of weight, flight design, and throwing technique.

Dart barrels are available in weights ranging from 11 grams to approximately 46 grams. To generalize again, lighter darts will tend to float to the board and strike the board with the tip angled downward. Heavier darts will tend to fly flatter or with the point angled upward and will enter the board in similar fashion.

There are three types of flight/shaft combinations. The first and traditionally the most popular is the feathered flight, which is marketed as a single flight/shaft unit. The feathered flight, made from turkey feathers (and folklore has it that only one set of three feathered flights can be gotten from an entire turkey), has three designs:

1. the standard feather
2. the full feather
3. the long feather.

Plastic flights are available in solid flight/shaft units and in the newer and increasingly popular "pop-off" polyvinyl flights to be used with slotted nylon or cane shafts. The latter flights can create an advantage for the accurate thrower. They offer little obstruction to a given throwing area, and when a dart with this flight design strikes the board very close to an existing dart in the board, the flight on the entering dart will pop off the shaft and permit the dart a straight line of entry.

Tom Barrett, the English champion, posits the argument that feathered flights are best when close grouping is called for. When struck by an incoming dart, he argues, the feathers on the dart in the board spread and allow the incoming dart a free line of flight. An argument against the pop-off flights is that, in fact, the flights pop off only after the incoming dart has already been diverted off its flight path. We take no stand on this issue but defer to personal preference. It seems that among the best players of the game feathered flights are still preferred. At the 1975 U.S. Masters, an invitational tournament consisting of the 32 finest players in the United States, 68 percent of the competing players used feather flights, 25 percent used a polyvinyl-flight/slotted-shaft combination, and 7 percent used either solid plastic flights or wooden darts.

Generally speaking—and again, other considerations being equal—flights that are greater in area will create more support for a dart in the air and toward the angle of entry. Flights with less area offer less support, and an underflighted dart will tend to strike the board in a submarine fashion with tip coming upward. Longer shafts also create more flight and entry support, while shorter shafts afford less flying support.

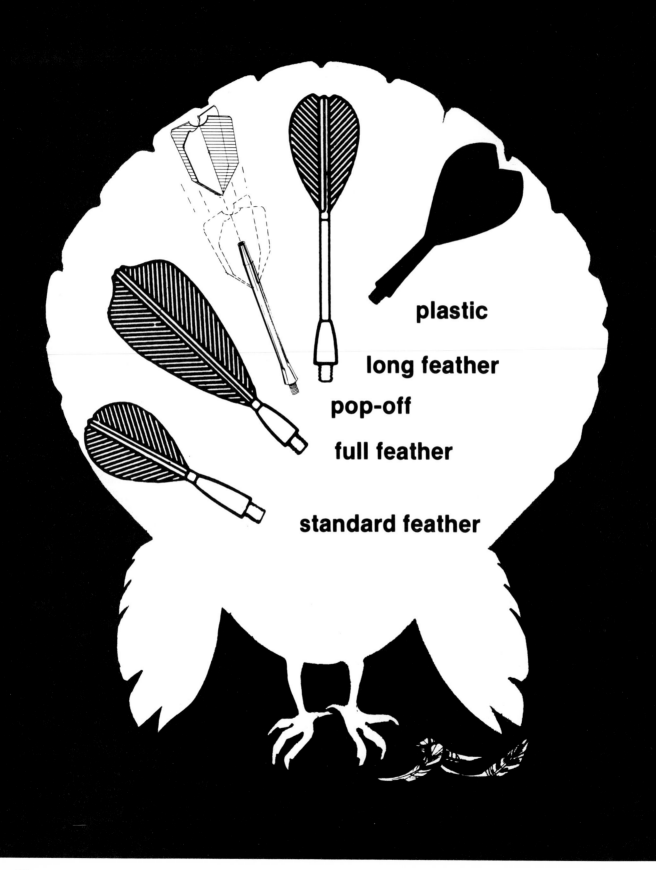

plastic

long feather

pop-off

full feather

standard feather

Longer shafts also create more flight and entry support, while shorter shafts afford less flying support.

With all these factors and considerations, the choice of a dart for any type of thrower is not an easy one. It is of prime importance that before any dart purchase is made, the dart being considered be thoroughly experimented with on a proper board and at the proper throwing distance. In this experimentation the following ought to be considered:

1. The general design and texture of the barrel. Does it feel comfortable in the thumb and fingertips? One barrel might do well for a two-finger grip but be unusable for a three or four-finger grip. Does the barrel have sufficient roughness and texture? All palms perspire in varying degrees and a very polished and slick barrel can be unusable in a paw that continually drips with perspiration.

2. The weight. Is it compatible with the speed and motion of the throw? Often, a hard thrower can do well with a slim, light dart. Here the speed of the throw will make up for the tendency of the light dart to float and strike the board at an imperfect angle. Similarly, a "bloop" type of throw might be complemented by a heavier dart. In this case the heavier dart will enter the board at a more perfect angle when "blooped" than will the lighter dart.

3. If a dart feels comfortable in terms of grip and weight but doesn't fly and enter well, the problem may be solved by an adjustment of flight and shaft. Thus, if a dart is consistently striking the board and falling away with tip up, this tendency might be remedied by adding greater flight area, i.e., replacing a standard feather flight with a full darrow-type feather. Or, if a dart tends to strike the board tip-down as it enters, a shorter shaft or smaller flight, or both, might be tried.

For years in the darts world the brass dart was king. Virtually all darts manufactured in the '30s, '40s, '50s, and '60s were made of brass. Some were silver or gold-plated, but still the basic material was brass. Recently there has been a revolution of sorts in the materials used in darts barrels. Barrels are now available in heavier, denser, and considerably more expensive metals, most notably tungsten alloy. Tungsten barrels offer definite advantages to the skilled player. Because of its greater metal density than brass, a tungsten barrel of a given weight has approximately one half the thickness of its brass counterpart. Three tungsten darts of medium weight (25 grams, for example) can easily nestle in the treble 20 bed, often with room for several friends, while three brass 25-grammers will be overcrowded and probably spilling into the treble 1 and treble 5 neighborhood.

Many serious players are now using tungsten arrows and probably all dart enthusiasts would use them if it were not for the price. A set of three tungsten alloy darts costs approximately $40–$50, while a set of three brassies can still be gotten for $5–$10.

There is one further type of dart that deserves mention. This is the wooden, or French, dart. This dart is rarely seen in pubs or in competition in England or America, as it simply doesn't fly as well as modern brass and tungsten arrows. However, darts rumor has it that there are still isolated pockets of French darts users and enthusiasts throughout the world.

The Dart Mat

The dart mat, a corrugated rubber strip approximately 10' long and 4' wide, is a common sight in pubs all over England. The mat is usually marked with three hockey lines, one at 8', one at 8'6", and one at 9', to accommodate the different throwing distances used in different pubs and regions. In all likelihood the mat will bear the shield and logo of a local brewery.

The mat, besides being decorative and an outlet for advertising, is quite functional as well. If used over a wooden floor, it will protect the floor from damage caused by darts that bounce out of the board and off of wires. In the case of a harder floor such as concrete or tile, the mat will serve to protect the dart points. A dart striking the thick corrugated mat will be undamaged, whereas a dart that strikes a concrete floor can be severely blunted.

Dart mats can be purchased for home use and can be a decorative and functional addition to a home darts salon, whether the salon is in actuality a free wall in the den or a cubbyhole next to the furnace. If the mat is an inconvenience in the family den, it can easily be rolled up when not in use.

The Scoreboard

There are several scoreboards used for scoring darts, the classic of which is the traditional chalkboard slate used in English pubs. The scoreboard is a must for pub and competitive play and can be a useful accessory in the home. Although other types of scoring boards are available (lucite models to be used with crayons or china markers, for example) we must admit a preference for the classic slate. After all, the phrase "Can I take the chalks?" rings with traditional flavor and darts etiquette. Somehow "Can I take the china marker?" doesn't carry the same meaning.

Dart-Board Cabinets

The double-door dart-board cabinet, as illustrated here, is another common sight in the English pub. This cabinet, like the dart mat, is decorative as

The Dart Board Cabinet (Granby, Inc., Santa Monica, California)

well as functional. First, it protects the wall area surrounding the board; second, it provides a very useful area for the scoring slate. For home use in the living room or den, for example, the cabinet when closed can appear to be an attractive wall decoration. Several designs of cabinets are available from suppliers in England and America. Most of these are quite expensive. The serious dart player with a minimum of carpentry skills should be able to construct an adequate and attractive cabinet for considerably less money.

Another type of dart-board enclosure used in pubs in England and America is the tire ring around the board. This is made by slitting an automobile tire in half to create a circular rubber backing against which the board is mounted. The tire enclosure is an interesting and attrative addition to the mounted board and is functional as well. It protects the wall area around the board and prevents darts that miss the board from being blunted. For those with an appreciation of culture and history, this mounting represents a pleasing combination of the old and the new: the game of darts as an historic working-class pastime encircled by a discarded appendage of the classic symbol of 20th-century technology, the automobile.

The Darts Case

Most sets of three darts are sold in a plastic case (or, if the purchase is Accudarts, a fine wooden case). The case is a convenience when transporting one's darts between home and pub. Furthermore, it will increase the life of shafts and flights, particularly feathered flights. Small leather darts pouches can also be used. The darts and shafts fit into one side of the pouch, while the folded polyvinyl flights are stored in a slot on the other side of the pouch. A slim pocket-size pouch such as this will encourage one to carry the darts at all times, and this practice is most strongly recommended.

Other Accessories

Other darts accessories include the dart sharpener and darts wax. The sharpener can be a very useful companion in the darts case. Sharp darts will glide around wires rather than bounce off them, and will decrease wear on the board. However, we have observed a few darters who sharpen their darts compulsively—after every trip to the hockey. It seems that these hurlers equate freshly sharpened arrows with throwing skill. No amount of sharpening can make up for poor throwing, yet we've seen several shooters who seem to sharpen their darts particularly vigorously after throwing a 26, as if somehow this score was the result of blunt darts.

Dart finger wax is a questionable accessory, to say the least. To gain a comfortable grip on the barrel of a dart, we have always preferred dampening the fingertips with the moisture from the outside of a draught of beer and then using a convenient drying agent, such as the seat of the pants. However, some players may feel more comfortable with a disc of finger wax; and although this may seem frivolous, if finger wax can help steer a dart into the treble 20, then we are all for it.

A final note on an accessory that, to date, does not exist, but one that would be of certain value to the darter who is very ill at ease with numbers and counting. As stressed on numerous occasions throughout this book, one of the key elements in successful darting is the ability to plan scoring strategies (and alternative scoring strategies in case of missed darts) while maintaining one's level of concentration during a three-dart throw. Unfortunately, this calls for certain mathematical skills, and equally unfortunately, some players, regardless of their throwing abilities, simply cannot cope with the mental mathematics necessary to instantly break down 74 into treble 14, double 16. Therefore we propose an accessory designed precisely for this player. The accessory is a pocket calculator that when fed a given number will read out a variety of three-dart and possibly two-dart finishes. Such a calculator is certainly technically feasible and, we suspect, would be quite marketable.

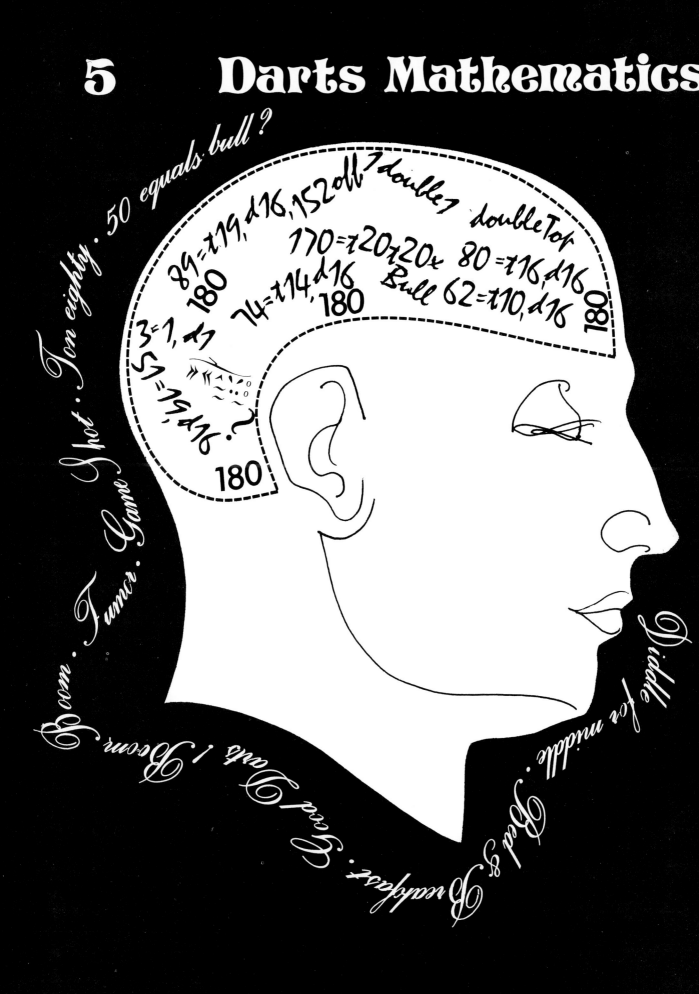

As we have said before, the ability to compute rapidly and plan and alter scoring strategies during a three-dart throw and while waiting for a turn to throw is an important element in playing competitive darts. This is particularly true when playing one of the standard games — "301," "501," etc.

The crucial scoring moment in terms of on-the-spot mathematical calculations is always near the end of a 301-type game. It is at this point that the expert coolly fires into an ideal closing double while the average player will fritter away at odd 30s and 20s. Although there are many charts that list possible two-dart and three-dart finishing strategies, we feel that they are not particularly useful to the average or even the good player. These charts are always made up for "ideal" finishes, which in many instances are simply beyond the capabilities of the less-than-expert player. Thus, while this kind of chart may list a three-dart finish from 121 as treble 17, double 15, double 20, this is not the best strategy for most darters.

We propose two charts: one for the expert player with all two- and three-dart ideal finishes from 170 downward, and one for the good and average player with two- and three-dart finishes from 100 downward. Included in this second chart will be notations indicating strategies and alternative strategies for the three-dart throw.

Before laying out these charts we will attempt to define what we mean by the terms "expert," "good," and "average."

The *expert* player is one who is a pub team player, a tournament player who in all likelihood has thrown several ton-eighties in his career and has the ability to regularly throw a game of "301" in 7 to 10 darts. For the expert player the opening double is rarely a problem, and any three-dart throw below 60 is a disappointment. In addition to the above, the expert is a very consistent thrower. Rarely, if ever, will he ruin an ideal closing double 16 by floating an arrow into the single 11 bed.

The *good* player also probably belongs to a local pub team, but is not of tournament playing caliber. The main difference between the expert and the good player is consistency. While the good player may be capable of a ton-eighty or a 152 off (double 16, treble 20, treble 20), he lacks consistency in the ability to score high regularly (60, 85, 100, etc.) in three darts, and to regularly open and finish the standard game. Perhaps another difference may be the ability to play well and consistently under pressure.

The average player probably struggles to get 20s and can only score in a desired double once every 15 to 20 darts. This is the player who has not yet developed the smooth rhythmic stroke necessary for pinpoint accurate throwing.

Expert Player's Chart

These are the ideal two and three-dart finishes from 170 downward, 170 being the maximum score possible on a three-dart throw ending with a double. The second and sometimes third strategies for a number are included for the player who might prefer a different starting treble or a closing double other than the first or second closing double indicated for a number. The center bull is indicated as a closing double in several instances.

Expert Player's Chart

170	t20	t20	Bull		138	t20	t18	d12
167	t19	t20	Bull		137	t19	t16	d16
164	t20	t18	Bull		136	t20	t20	d8
161	t17	t20	Bull		135	t20	t15	d15
160	t20	t20	d20			t20	t19	d9
158	t20	t20	d19			t20	t13	d18
157	t19	t20	d20		134	t20	t14	d16
156	t20	t20	d18		133	t20	t19	d8
155	t20	t19	d19		132	t20	t16	d12
154	t18	t20	d20			t20	t18	d9
153	t20	t19	d18		131	t20	t13	d16
152	t20	t20	d16		130	t20	d15	d20
151	t17	t20	d20			t20	t18	d8
150	t20	t18	t18		129	t19	d18	d18
149	t19	t20	d16			t19	t12	d18
148	t20	t16	d20			t20	t15	d12
147	t20	t17	d18		128	t20	t20	d4
146	t20	t18	d16		127	t20	t17	d8
145	t20	t15	d20		126	t20	d15	d18
	t20	t19	d14			t20	16	d9
144	t20	t20	d12		125	t20	25	d20
	t20	t16	d18			t20	t11	d16
143	t20	t17	d16		124	t20	t16	d8
142	t20	t14	d20		123	t19	t14	d12
	t20	t18	d14			t19	t10	d18
141	t20	t19	d12		122	t20	d15	d16
	t20	t15	d18			t20	t10	d16
140	t20	t16	d16		121	t17	d15	d20
139	t19	t14	d20			t19	t16	d8
	t20	t13	d20		120	t20	20	d20
	t20	t17	d14		119	t19	d15	d16

	t19	t10	d16	95	t19	d19
118	t20	18	d20	94	t18	d20
117	t19	20	d20	93	t19	d18
116	t20	16	d20	92	t20	d16
	t20	20	d18	91	t17	d20
115	t19	18	d20	90	t18	d18
114	t20	18	d18	89	t19	d16
	t20	14	d20	88	t16	d20
113	t19	16	d20	87	t17	d18
	t19	20	d18	86	t18	d16
112	t20	20	d16	85	t15	d20
111	t17	20	d20		t19	d14
	t19	18	d18	84	t20	d12
110	t20	18	d16		t16	d18
	t20	Bull		83	t17	d16
109	t19	20	d16	82	t14	d20
108	t20	16	d16		t20	d11
107	t19	18	d16	81	t19	d12
106	t20	14	d16		t15	d18
105	t15	20	d20	80	t16	d16
	t19	16	d16	79	t17	d14
104	t18	18	d16		t19	d11
	t20	12	d16		t13	d20
103	t17	20	d16	78	t18	d12
	t19	14	d16		t20	d9
102	t20	10	d16		t14	d18
101	t17	18	d16	77	t19	d10
	t19	12	d16		t15	d16
100	t20	d20		76	t20	d8
99	t19	10	d16	75	t19	d9
98	t20	d19			t17	d12
97	t19	d20			t13	d18
96	t20	d18		74	t14	d16

73	t19	d8		t15	d8
72	12	d18	60	20	d20
	t18	d9	59	19	d20
	t16	d12	58	18	d20
71	t13	d16	57	17	d20
70	t10	d20	56	16	d20
	t18	d8		20	d18
69	t19	d6	55	15	d20
	t17	d9	54	14	d20
68	t20	d4		18	d18
	t12	d16	53	13	d20
67	t17	d8	52	20	d16
66	t10	d18	51	19	d16
	t16	d9	50	18	d16
65	t11	d16		Bull	
	25	d20	49	17	d16
	t19	d4	48	16	d16
64	t16	d8	47	15	d16
63	t19	d2	46	14	d16
	t15	d9	45	13	d16
	t13	d12	44	12	d16
62	t10	d16	43	11	d16
	t18	d4	42	10	d16
61	t19	d2	41	9	d16

General Strategies

In almost all instances the closing double indicated is an even-number double. This is to ensure that after a missed double shot in which the single of the desired double is scored, the remaining score will be even and the game can still be won in one dart. The double 16 appears as the final closing double in the majority of instances for this very reason. Assuming a miss into the single scoring area, double 16 becomes double 8, double 4, double 2, and if there is a miss at this point, the shooter deserves double 1.

For several numbers (130, 129, 126, 122, 121, 119) a double shot is indicated for the second dart. This is a particularly difficult shot. The missed double can yield no score at all, or the single of the number, both of which are undesirable.

Good or Average Player's Chart

In many instances, as in the expert's chart, alternatives are listed for players who might prefer one closing double over another, or a given treble or single number on the first or second dart over another. The listings below a three-dart finish for a number (and marked by an asterisk*) indicate alternative strategies should there be a miss on the first or second dart.

Good or Average Player's Chart

170-100 — We suggest that between this range the first dart always be thrown at the treble 20, or if the shooter prefers the lower side of the board, treble 19. If the score is very close to 100, the wise player will shoot treble 19 with an odd score remaining and treble 20 with an even score remaining.

100	t20, d20	91	t17, d20
	*20, t16, d16		*17, t14, d16
	*20, 16, t16 leaves d8		*17, 14, 20 leaves d20
			t19, d17
99	t19, 10, d16		*19, t18, d9
	*19, t16, d16		*19, 18, 14 leaves d20
	*19, 16, t16 leaves d8		
		90	t18, d18
98	t20, d19		*18, t18, d9
	*20, t20, d9		*18, 18, 18 Leaves d18
	*20, 20, 18 leaves d20		t20, d15
			*20, t18, d8
97	t19, d20		*20, 18, 20 leaves d16
	*19, t20, d9		
	*19, 20, 18 leaves d20	89	t19, d16
			*19, t18, d8
96	t20, d18		*19, 18, 20 leaves d16
	*20, t20, d8		
	*20, 20, 16 leaves d20	88	t20, d14
			*20, t12, d16
95	t19, d19		*20, 12, 16 leaves d20
	*19, t20, d8		t16, d20
	*19, 20, 16 leaves d20		*16, t18, d9
			*16, 18, 14 leaves d20
94	t18, d20		
	*18, t20, d8	87	t19, d15
	*18, 20, 16 leaves d20		*19, t20, d4
	t20, d17		*19, 20, 16 leaves d16
	*20, t14, d16		t17, d18
	*20, 14, 20 leaves d20		*17, t18, d8
			*17, 18, 20 leaves d16
93	t19, d18		
	*19, t14, d16	86	t18, d16
	*19, 14, 20 leaves d20		*18, t20, d4
			*18, 20, 14 leaves d16
92	t20, d16		
	*20, t18, d9	85	t19, d14
	*20, 18, 14 leaves d20		

	*19, t16, d9	75	t19, d9
	*19, 16, 18 leaves d16		*19, 16, d20
	t17, d17		t17, d12
	*17, t12, d16		*17, 18, d20
	*17, 12, 14, leaves d20	74	t14, d16
	t15, d20		*14, 20, d20
	*15, t18, d8		t18, d10
	*15, 18, 20 leaves d16		*18, 20, d16
84	t20, d12	73	t19, d8
	*20, t16, d8		*19, 14, d20
	*20, 16, 16 leaves d16	72	t20, d6
83	t17, d16		*20, 20, d16
	*17, t16, d9		t18, d9
	*17, 16, 18 leaves d16		*18, 18, d18
	t19, d13		t12, d18
	*19, t16, d8		*12, 20, d20
	*19, 16, 16 leaves d16	71	t13, d16
82	t20, d6		*13, 18, d20
	*20, t10, d16		t17, d10
	*20, 10, 20 leaves d16		*17, 18, d18
	t18, d14	70	t18, d8
	*18, t16, d8		*18, 20, d16
	*18, 16, 16 leaves d16		t10, d20
81	t19, d12		*10, 20, d20
	*19, t10, d16	69	t19, d6
	*19, 10, 20 leaves d16		*19, 18, d16
80	t20, d10		*19, Bull
	*20, 20, d20		t15, d12
	t16, d16		*15, 14, d20
	*16, t16, d8	68	t12, d16
	*16, 16, 16 leaves d16		*12, 16, d20
79	t19, d11		t20, d4
	*19, 20, d20		*20, 16, d16
78	t20, d9	67	t17, d8
	*20, 18, d20		*17, 18, d16
	t18, d12		*17, Bull
	*18, 20, d20	66	t10, d18
77	t19, d10		*10, 16, d20
	*19, 18, d20		18, 16, d16
	t17, d13	65	t11, d16
	*17, 20, d20		*11, 14, d20
	t15, t10, d16		t19, d4
	*15, 10, 20 leaves d20		*19, 14, d16
76	t20, d8		17, 16, d16
	*20, 16, d20		

64	t16, d8		53	13, d20
	*16, 16, d16		52	20, d16
63	t17, d6		51	19, d16
	*17, 14, d16		50	18, d16
62	t10, d16			Bull
	*10, 20, d16		49	17, d16
61	t19, d2		48	16, d16
	*19, 10, d16		47	15, d16
60	20, d20		46	14, d16
59	19, d20		45	13, d16
58	18, d20		44	12, d16
57	17, d20		43	11, d16
56	16, d20		42	10, d16
55	15, d20		41	9, d16
54	14, d20			
	18, d18			

Specific Strategies

This second chart is virtually identical to the expert player's chart in terms of the initial three- and two-dart strategies. The basic difference is the inclusion in the second chart of alternative strategies based on a miss of the first or second dart. The thrower following this chart should anticipate these alternatives before throwing. In this way, concentration can be maintained at the hockey line, and the player will stand a greater chance of maneuvering to the ideal closing double.

To the beginner, either of these charts may seem formidable; indeed, both are, to some extent, geared to top-class play. A treble 20, treble 17, and double 16 finish in three darts is formidable play in any company. It would be a bold and confident player who would aim to finish 65 with a treble 11, double 16. The average player with two darts left might be inclined to throw at the 19 bed with a single 19, leaving 46. The second dart would be aimed at the 14 to leave double 16. (Of course, should a treble 19 be scored with the first dart, this will leave a double 4, a makable even-number double.) This may be a reasonable strategy in the average game, especially where the opponent may be some distance behind, but the good player—and certainly the top tournament player—will aim to finish the game as quickly as possible, rather than set himself up for the next throw. He will know that his opponent, even if he has a three-figure number, may well finish in his next throw.

While certain finishes have a flamboyant air (the use of the inner and outer bull is always suitable only for the expert), there is no reason why the average player should not follow the strategies suggested in the charts. Indeed, there are positive reasons why he should. In the first case, even if he is not likely to achieve a particular finish, he should still aim at it. The average golfer, faced with a six iron to the green, may well fluff the shot and fall short. He would be foolish, however, to take a four iron and assume he will have a miss hit. In darts, as in many games, it is good advice, if it is "on," to go for it. Also, in most cases, there is nothing to be lost, and something to be gained, by following the strategy of the top players. It should be noted that, in each case where a treble is called for, a single will at least leave the player on an even number and on his road to a double. Let us take an example: A player on 80 with two darts left and thinking conservatively may aim to throw two 20s, leaving himself with double 20 on his next throw. He runs two risks in doing this. First, he might shoot a treble 20 with his second dart and be "bust" back to 80. Second, he may allow his opponent to win on his next throw. If the strategy of the charts is adopted, he will aim at treble 16. Even if he gets only two singles, he will be left with the useful 48 (all the 16s) on his next throw. He will have "warmed up" on the 16s and will probably be just as likely to go out on that as on the double 20, side doubles being generally easier than top doubles for the average player. Furthermore, should he score single 16, he will be left with double 8.

As we hinted before, a player should not only have a clear idea of what he aims to achieve but a range of alternate strategies should he fail. In his book *Darts,* the English champion Tom Barrett makes the useful suggestion that the player should make a note of the numbers adjacent to his particular target and be clear about what he will do should he hit one of these numbers. Suppose a player is left with 89 and is aiming at a treble 19, double 16 finish. Let us suppose he is good enough not to throw wider than the 3 bed or 7 bed in shooting treble 19 with the first dart. In this case, the possible numbers he will hit on the first dart, aside from the desired treble 19, are single 19, double 19, single 7, double 7, treble 7, single 3, double 3, and treble 3. Each of these numbers offers a two- or three-dart finish as follows:

1. Single 19 leaves 70, 2nd dart at treble 10 leaving double 20.
2. Double 19 leaves 51, 2nd dart at 19 leaving double 16.
3. Single 7 leaves 82, 2nd dart at treble 14 leaving double 20.
4. Treble 7 leaves 68, 2nd dart at treble 20 leaving double 4.
5. Double 7 leaves 75, 2nd dart at treble 19 leaving double 9.
6. Single 3 leaves 86, 2nd dart at treble 18 leaving double 16.
7. Treble 3 leaves 80, 2nd dart at treble 16 leaving double 16.
8. Double 3 leaves 83, 2nd dart at treble 17 leaving double 16.

Obviously these eight possibilities cannot be committed to memory for every conceivable shot. However, the experienced player has learned to become familiar with certain combinations and recurring patterns, especially with those numbers in the 90s, 80s, 70s, and 60s that can be reduced to double 16 or double 20 by shooting a high treble. A simple mathematical formula can be applied here. First, one should become very familiar with the score values of all the high trebles, thus:

$$t20 = 60$$
$$t19 = 57$$
$$t18 = 54$$
$$t17 = 51$$
$$t16 = 48$$
$$t15 = 45$$
$$t14 = 42$$
$$t13 = 39$$
$$t12 = 36$$

To quickly calculate a finish, a given score is reduced by 32 (double 16) or 40 (double 20), and if the resulting number is one of the treble score values, then the first dart to be thrown is determined. In some instances, the score should be reduced by 16 (double 8) or 8 (double 4) to determine the treble.

Specifically, these numbers are 76, 73, 70, 68, 67, 65, and 64. It can be noted that over 50 percent of the time a score between 62 and 100 can be reduced to a double 20 or double 16 by throwing a high treble.

If the score, when reduced by 32 or 40, does not equal a treble, there are two choices. First, the player can go for a high treble, knowing that the treble, if scored, will leave a less-than-desirable double. For example, with 87 left, shoot treble 19, double 15 or treble 17, double 18. It should be remembered that a high odd number below 99 can always be reduced to a double by shooting a high odd treble, and a high even number from 100 downwards can be similarly reduced by shooting a high even treble.

Second, the player can opt to go for score on a single number and work his way into an ideal double. Thus, to come down from 87 means shooting 19 (to get even), treble 20, double 4 or 19, treble 12, double 16.

These choices depend on a player's confidence in getting a given treble and closing with an unusual double. The choice might also be determined by the closeness of a particular match. In a close match, or in a match in which the opponent is already shooting for a double, the first alternative (going for a high treble and an unusual double) should be considered. However, in a match where the opponent is far behind in score or not even away, the safer strategy — going for a high single number score to work toward a double 16 or double 20 — should be employed.

6 The Undiscovered History

Darts has no history. This is not to deny that the throwing of darts is a most ancient activity indeed and that by various stages it developed into the modern game. But as the historian E. H. Carr observed: "Not all facts about the past are facts of history." It is the historian who turns facts into history and in the case of darts he has chosen not to do so. Even the evolution of the modern game, taking place in little more than the last hundred years, has gone unrecorded. The origins of the games played and the peculiar structure of the board remain a mystery.

It may be objected that the historian has more important things to do — that he should go about his business of dealing with significant social and political events and not concern himself with something that is, after all, only a game, merely a way of passing the time. But how we choose to pass the time may have its own significance. What people choose to do in their leisure hours outside the enforced periods of work may tell us something about the quality of their lives, about their relationship to the world of work, and about the satisfactions they seek in the realm of play. Leisure activities carry with them a set of values and attitudes, an implied code of behavior, a special language, and an appropriate style. They are part of our culture.

This anthropological notion of culture as a whole way of life, central to discussions about mass and popular culture, was promoted by, among others, T. S. Eliot. It is worth quoting Eliot on the matter if only because he makes a reference, not unsurprisingly, to the game of darts:

> The reader must remind himself, as the author has constantly to do, of how much is here embraced by the term *culture*. It includes all the characteristic activities and interests of a people: Derby Day, Henley Regatta, Cowes, the twelfth of August, a cup final, the dog races, the pin table, the dart board, Wensleydale cheese, boiled cabbage cut into sections, beetroot in vinegar, nineteenth-century Gothic churches and the music of Elgar.

The American reader, to whom this list may seem somewhat esoteric, can find American equivalents: hamburgers with coleslaw and french fries, the bowling alley, the blues, McDonald's hamburger stands, pompom girls, the architecture of Chicago, the World Series, and so on.

In America, darts has yet to become absorbed into this mainstream culture and may best be regarded as a subculture. Indeed, this would also be so in England. Darts is, and despite some pressures to the contrary, remains, a working-class activity. Eliot's list is a product of his conservatism, his belief in tradition and the myth of the organic community. It is obvious that the ladies and gentlemen who sail at Cowes or celebrate the twelfth of August by traveling to Scotland to shoot wild animals do not afterwards dash off to the local pub to sink a couple of pints and have a few quick games of "301." On the other hand, those returning from the dog races or the Cup Final are most likely to do just that.

Statistics for leisure-time activities are always problematic, and estimates vary; but it seems likely that in England today, outside of working and sleeping, more people spend more time playing darts than doing anything else. The only possible exceptions would be fishing or making love. Such a phenomenon calls for attention. The time is ripe. Darts is at present going through the phase that overtakes all such pastimes, of passing from a casual game with its local rules to a codified, regulated, and commercially promoted national and international sport. Hopefully some interested historian of working-class culture will turn his attention to this before it is too late.

There do exist many commendable histories of sports, games, and pastimes; but few make anything more than a mere passing reference to darts — and that never to the growth of the modern game but to some ancient and obscure antecedent. Those activities that receive most attention can be divided into two classes. The first and most significant are those associated with the military and with royalty. The two, of course, are interrelated. Training in a military skill was frequently a Court pastime and as such is of interest to the historian concerned with the traditional issues of politics and war. One such pastime, archery, (whose history is well recorded), is a good example, and most books on the subject refer to medieval edicts designed to encourage practice in the use of the longbow and discourage other less useful activities. Along with archery, other "exercises practiced by persons of rank," such as hawking, have reasonably full historical accounts.

The other class of activities that have secured some attention are the popular entertainments of the people, which include spectacles, festivities, and performances such as the Miracle Plays, jugglers, and dancing bears, as well as games such as early forms of bowling, skittles, etc. Interest here is generated, on the one hand, by the social and religious function of these activities and, on the other, by the fact that many of these pastimes have not survived into the contemporary world. Much of the study of folk activities is motivated by nostalgia, a desire to picture a way of life in which the folk amused themselves by taking part in simple communal activities — a picture invariably set against the notion of urban man passively receiving his diet of mechanized pap. This is no place to pursue the argument, except to note that it is wholly at variance with the facts, but such an attitude among those interested in recording the leisure-time activities of a people might account, in part, for the neglect of darts.

While rural inns in England have had, and many still do have, their dart board, the modern game has been developed primarily as part of urban working-class culture. Also it is not a dying game. On the contrary, it flourishes and, while its traditions are under pressure from rapid change, it has none of the romantic allure of decay.

Darts is both a very ancient game and a modern one. One of the main tasks of the historian would be to fill in the gap between these two. A dart is a combination of spear and arrow. As such its primitive origins are to be found in hunting and warfare. As we have suggested, many of the games and pastimes of medieval England (and indeed of other peoples going back to the most ancient times) were derived from these functional activities and were often rehearsals or training for them.

A useful source of information on these early games from which darts emerged is *The Sports and Pastimes of the People of England,* by Joseph Strutt, first published in 1801. A great variety of games existed involving the casting of stones and bars, the throwing of the hammer and the javelin, etc. These games divided into two kinds: those designed to test strength and those testing accuracy. The most obvious source of darts is of course archery, with its arrow, its feathered flight, and its characteristic target. An echo of this remains today inasmuch as it is not unusual for an English player to refer to his darts as his arrows. Alongside the butts for archery practice, other targets existed, most notably the quintain used for the lance. At the same time smaller arrows, designed to be flung by the hand, had been developed for use by English archers in close fighting. It was the combination of these elements that led to the emergence of the game referred to as *dartes* by early chroniclers.

At this point the references are tantalizingly brief. The ambassador of Charles V to the court of Henry VIII wrote in 1532 that Anne Boleyn had presented Henry with certain *dartes* "of Biscayan fashion richly ornamented." Froissart's *Chronicles* mention the fact that Charles VI of France and his court were amused by "wrestling and casting of the bar and darte by Frenchmen and the Gascoyns." Vernon Bartlett, an English writer, in his book *The Past of Pastimes,* refers to the fact that the French historian, Paul Pelissen, while in the Bastille in the seventeenth century, amused himself by making and playing darts — although his real claim to fame was that he tamed a spider. It is also frequently said that some of the Pilgrim Fathers whiled away their lonely days on the Mayflower by playing the game of darts. However, these and other tales do not take us very far. Whatever game was being played in those far-off days bears little relationship to the game as we know it today, beyond the basic concept of throwing a dart at a target. We can be certain that the palace halls did not resound to cries of "mugs away" or "bust" as Anne and Henry went through a game of "301" and that the beams of the Mayflower did not carry charts showing the Fathers how to go out in three darts from 144.

The Modern Game I—Beginnings

The growth of the modern game can be divided into three phases: 1. the period of nineteenth-century evolution; 2. the period of growing popularity in the first half of the twentieth century; 3. the contemporary period of international growth.

As already noted the first phase is virtually undocumented. It is characterized by the development of the game in the English Inn, the evolution of new boards similar to the standard board in use today, the production of short, light darts, and the emergence of the basic "301" game. The development is logical. Once inside the tavern the throw had to be shorter, which in turn demanded a more difficult scoring area than that provided by the simple archery target. Exactly how it took its present form is not known. Early boards were made of wood, and indeed to this day the famous *News of the World* Championship, long the premier championship in the darts world, favors the wooden (elm) board. It has been suggested that the segments and the treble and double rings of the modern board were derived from the concentric rings on these early log-end boards plus the cracks and splits that come with aging.

In these early days, darts merely took its place alongside many other pub games, such as the now vanishing Shove Ha'penny. It had no great popularity and certainly no national competitions. As a result there were considerable local variations in games, rules, and equipment. This is still evident in the rubber dart mats produced in England, which are marked off in a variety of throwing distances to suit local needs. Although they shared the basic segmented pattern, a great variety of boards also existed in different parts of the country. Presumably these boards were handmade within their own regions by local craftsmen. Some have vanished but others are still in use, and players in some regions cling to their own board despite pressure to adopt the board now standard for national and international competition. To this day, Nodor, a major manufacturer, still makes seven different types of board. It seems worth offering a brief description of these boards:

The Yorkshire Board

Used in parts of Kent as well as Yorkshire, this board is the same as the standard but lacks the 25 and the trebles ring.

The Irish Board

This is the same as the Yorkshire except that it is all black. This makes it more difficult to see the divisions, which is either a piece of Irish whimsy or a deliberate incitement to an argument.

The Burton Board

The same as the standard but without trebles and 25. Its distinguishing feature is the presence of two diamond shapes outside the numbers, each counting 25. Used around Burton-upon-Trent.

The Lincoln

This board has no trebles or 25, but the playing area is larger than the standard. Used around the city of Lincoln as well as in some places on the Medway.

Wide Fives

The most distinctive of boards, it has only twelve segments and uses only the numbers 5, 10, 15, and 20. It has doubles, trebles, a bull, and a 25. A variation of this board has doubles and trebles almost as narrow as the wire itself. The Fives board is still popular in the east end of London.

We have given this brief description of different boards because darts players visiting England might find it interesting to visit some of the areas where these regional boards are still in use. They will not be in use much longer. Perhaps some enterprising and wealthy darts enthusiasts might consider setting up a darts museum so that these and other examples of early equipment might be preserved.

Early darts were of a very simple design, basically a wooden barrel, a metal point, and feathered flights. Various refinements were added, such as a metal ring for weighting. It was not, however, until after the turn of the century that darts with an all-metal barrel were produced.

One of the few early concrete references to the modern game is recorded by Tom Barrett in his book *Darts*. For long periods, games of chance were illegal in public houses. In 1908 "Foot" Anakin, a landlord of a pub in Leeds, was brought before the magistrate's court charged with running a game of chance, namely darts. Foot's defense was to ask permission to have a dart board set up in court to demonstrate that darts was a game of considerable skill. Permission

N.D.A. No. 2 " B " pattern,
Yorkshire, Kent.

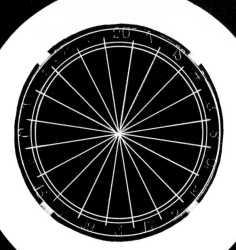

Lincoln, Medway
(15 inch playing area)

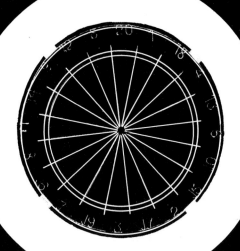

Irish board, Irish all black.

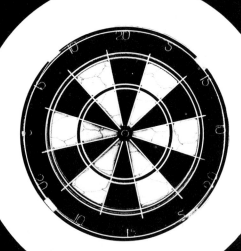

Wide fives, London
fives, Ipswich

Burton board.

Narrow fives,
competition fives

was granted and, in a contest with a junior clerk, Foot shot a series of double 20s and won his case.

By the time that Foot Anakin gave his famous demonstration, the basics of modern darts, in terms of the games and equipment, had been established. As we have seen, however, there were many regional variations, and while most areas had their enthusiasts, there was no national following.

Stanley Lowy, the managing director of Unicorn, one of the largest of modern darts manufacturers, has confirmed the legend (cited earlier in this book) that it was his father who first conceived the idea of putting a set of three darts into one box. Previously they had been sold singly through small stores. This was as late as the mid-1930s.

The Modern Game II—The Age of Popularity

The popular phase of the game in England begins with World War I and extends in a constantly rising curve through World War II and the years following. These years saw more and more people playing the game, more leagues being organized, more competitions being promoted, and the formation of the National Darts Association of Great Britain. The middle '30s also saw the publication of the first books on darts, most of them confusingly called *Darts* and now out of print. The first book seems to have been that by R. Croft-Cooke, published in 1936. It still remains one of the best about the ambience of the game.

The game's historically most famous competition, the *News of the World* Championship, also had its origins in these years. The *News of the World* is a mass-circulation Sunday newspaper that brings heady Sunday-morning reading to the British public. The basis of its appeal rests on its reporting of court cases involving divorce and those characteristically English sex crimes that expose shady vicars, defrocked priests, and down-at-the-heels ex-army officers. It also has a well-documented sports section and for years was active in the sponsorship of a variety of sporting events, the most notable of which was golf's British Match Play Championship. In 1927 the newspaper sponsored an individual darts championship confined to the London area. There were over 1,000 entrants. Throughout the '30s the competition grew and by 1938 it involved the whole of England and Wales in six regional championships. On the eve of war, over 14,000 spectators gathered to see the London and Southern England Finals being played. In the 1947/48 season it was decided to bring the regional winners together for a grand final to produce the *News of the World* Champion. It is a unique feature of this event that anyone can enter. The playoff rounds are arranged through the network of small leagues in local areas leading up to the regional tournaments. In the postwar years Scotland and Eire were added as regions and in the '70s the Championship took on an international character with the addition of the open champions of Sweden and the U.S.A. America was represented in 1973 and 1974 by Al Lippman from Philadelphia and in 1975 by Conrad Daniels from New Jersey.

The finals are held in the vast Alexandra Palace on a hill in north London overlooking the city. Some 500,000 enter the *News of the World* and the figure grows each year. The games are played on the traditional wooden boards of beautifully finished elm. In addition to the thousands who come to see the finals, there are now added millions who see it on television. For years the

 NEWS OF THE WORLD

DART COMPETITIONS.

DOGGER BANK No. 1 TEAM,

Winners of 2 Silver Cups and Several other Prizes.

organization of this mammoth event has been handled by Doris Williams, a quiet, modest lady, working in a section of a small office in the newspaper headquarters.

The *News of the World* Championship has recently become somewhat overshadowed by other more widely publicized events with greater awards. Nevertheless it remains a prestige Championship. The competition is intense. Many great players are eliminated in the early stages. Merely to reach the final is the mark of a player of the highest class.

The history of darts to this point is inevitably that of the history of the game in England. Of course, darts in one form or another has been played in America, as in other English-speaking countries, for almost as long as it has been played in England. But the true game was played only by a handful of enthusiasts in bars in New York, San Francisco, and a few other centers. To the world at large, if darts meant anything, it was a game for children. In the book *Social Games and Recreations,* published in 1935, there is a description of how to make a darts board. The bull has a diameter of three inches and a series of circles measure one and one-half inches across. The suggested throw is 15 to 20 feet.

Even in the late '60s there was only one bar in Chicago with a dart board. Today there are scores, with a network of leagues and competitions. Darts as a national sport in America began to emerge in the '60s, but the real and rapid growth has been in the '70s. This brings us to the third phase of the development of the game.

The Modern Game III—An International Sport

This third phase of the game, which is in progress, is characterized by the standardization of equipment and rules, commercial sponsorship, the promotion of international competition, and the emergence of superstars.

Each of these developments is bound up with the other. Increasing competition at the national level inevitably led to standardization and the erosion of the regional games. The growing popularity of the game attracts sponsors, which in turn leads to more ambitious competitions with greater awards. In consequence, competition becomes more intense, standards rise, and there emerges a group of stars at the national and even the international level. Out of this interaction comes a complex of tournaments and tournament players, exhibition matches, managers, agents, and a new breed of darts entrepreneur.

The first sign of this development is the emergence of star players. Darts enthusiasts are familiar with the sets of darts now promoted in association with the names of such contemporary players as Bob Thiede and Alan Evans. But the practice dates some way back. By popular agreement, the first two stars of the darts world were the Englishmen, Joe Hitchcock and Jim Pike. In a quite early paperback edition of Croft-Cooke's *Darts* (originally published in 1936), an advertisement announces a set of darts "as used by Joe Hitchcock." Pike and Hitchcock were in their heyday in the years immediately following World War II. They led outstanding teams and their own high skills set standards for younger players then emerging. Both lost their amateur status. Pike turned to work on the music-hall circuit and Hitchcock joined the staff of Watney's (the brewers), giving exhibitions. These two were experts at the trick shot, such as extinguishing a lit match held between the teeth or dislodging a coin from behind some trusting person's ear. They could throw four-inch nails better than most people could throw darts. It is recorded that in one game played with nails, Hitchcock went straight out from 130, scoring 60, 20, and 50.

This standard of play stimulated competition in those postwar years. Top-class players began to play for the same teams, often traveling some distance to do so. The result was the domination of leagues by a small number of teams. As a consequence, some of the leagues collapsed. There were also attempts to exclude these expert players from normal local competitions, combined with charges of professionalism. As a result there arose the conception of the super league, the first of which was the Greater London Super League, formed in the 1966/67 season. This is the beginning of the third phase of the development of the game. The super league existed above the grass-roots level of the game and was based on the idea that players could rise to a higher class, as happens in professional sports. This in turn led to more competitive play and more sponsorship. The sponsors included brewers like Watney's and tobacco firms like John Players but also, most notably, darts equipment manufacturers like Nodor and Unicorn. These developments had bypassed the somewhat conservative and grass-roots oriented National Darts Association, and a new body, the British Darts Organisation, was set up. The BDO aims to promote darts as a national and international sport, minimize its working-class origins and beer-swilling atmosphere, and find new sponsors. The ultimate mecca is of course television, where darts will take its place alongside, if not equal to, the gold mines of tennis and other sports.

A similar development under different conditions has taken place in the United States. The United States Darting Association was formed in 1969. It has run a number of tournaments, most notably the United States Open, finding sponsorship from whiskey firms such as Jameson's and Black and White. It was never a grass-roots body, nor could it have been, and the U.S. Open was never organized with the structure of area and regional playoffs like the *News of the World.* In the meantime the popularity of the game had grown rapidly and a network of small leagues mushroomed throughout the country. These had little relationship to each other or to the USDA. At the same time there grew up some large area organizations such as the Southern California Darts Association and the Greater New York Darts League, and new regional tournaments offering quite substantial prize money. It is in this context that a new body, the American Darts Organization, was set up in late 1975. It has proposed a structure of eight regions covering the whole country, with elected regional representatives. The ADO is a parallel body to the British Darts Organisation and would seem to have similar aims and aspirations. These changes have taken place in an atmosphere of very active promotion by the darts manufacturing companies. The USDA has links with Darts Unlimited and through them to the Kwiz Company, while Unicorn has given support to both the ADO and the BDO. Unicorn has been especially active in promoting the game outside England, most notably in Sweden; the company already exports to eighty different countries.

In 1974 Britain exported $4,800,000 worth of darts equipment. This was a 43 percent increase over 1973 and represented a not insignificant proportion of the country's exports of sports equipment. Also growing are the tournaments—in numbers, scope, and prize money offered. Each year there are

Part of the audience at the 1975 *News of the World* Darts Championship

regular tournaments held in different parts of this continent—the Northern American Open (organized by the California Darts Association), the Canadian Klondyke Open, and the Michigan Open—with prize money ranging from $4,000 to $30,000. This is small beer compared to the golf or tennis circuit but it is a remarkable advance for a game that did not exist as a national sport a few years ago. These tournaments increasingly take on an international character. Recently Stefan Lord from Sweden won the Santa Monica Open and Conrad Daniels from America appeared on the British TV program *The Indoor League*. Regularly national teams compete against each other in America, England, Sweden, and Canada, bringing with them managers and troops of supporters. The international growth of the game began, naturally, in the English-speaking countries and in those territories once governed by Britain. The game is now being played in many countries outside these boundaries. We have already noted how it thrives in Sweden, but significantly a Japanese Darts Association was recently formed. An article in the English journal *Darts World* recorded how the serious Japanese darts player prepares for his game by going into a retreat for muscle-toning exercises, vegetarian meals, posture training, and Zen meditation. A Japanese darts master urges players not to think of the board, the target, or techniques, but rather to concentrate on inner tranquillity: "The dart is propelled on its pre-determined path by the player's spirit or soul in harmony with the total environment." The English player aims to arrive at the same state by drinking several pints of beer.

Perhaps the most ambitious tournament in terms of organization and international character is the Unicorn World Championship, a competition for teams of two from different countries. In organizing this for the 1976 event, Unicorn has worked with the British Darts Organisation and the American Darts Organization. In Britain there exists a complex network of playoffs to determine the regional champions and then the national champions. As we

The Electronic scoreboard at Alexandra Palace, London

write, regional tournaments are being held in six different centers as a step toward determining which pair shall represent America in the finals to be held in London and covered by live television. It is expected that teams from seventeen countries will take part.

It is difficult to assess these various developments, especially as this third phase of the game's history is just under way. This is particularly true in the United States, where changes have taken place in a hothouse atmosphere. At one level we have the emergence of a group of tournament players, a small elite group who travel nationally and internationally playing in tournaments, giving exhibitions, and usually having links with one or another of the commercial manufacturers, endorsing and promoting their goods. Obviously this blurs the old distinction between amateur and professional. On the whole, this issue has been evaded for good and sensible reasons but does now and then surface, as in recent accusations that there have been attempts to exclude two international players from the *News of the World* Championship. The pattern is, of course, familiar in other sports and it is possible that darts will go the way of track and tennis and develop a professional wing.

At the level of organization it is not clear what view the ADO will take of emerging professionalism or what its relationship will be, or should be, to the existing grass-roots structure. In England the BDO is about to enter into discussions with the National Darts Association with a view to a merger. This issue of having two national organizations is less of a problem in America because the USDA is relatively new and does not have deep roots in the regions.

One thing can be said: the growth of national and international competition has led to a remarkably high standard of play among the top players. For those unfamiliar with play at this level, it ought to be useful to quote one example at random. In a recent game of "1001," Alan Glazier, the English player, went out as follows: 100, 140, 180, 140, 180, 180, 81. It is also remarkable how quickly American players have caught up with this kind of standard.

What is regarded as the first meeting between the United States and Britain took place in October 1972 with Bob Thiede, Jack Carr, and Jacqueline Egan representing the U.S.A. Britain won this first encounter. However, in a match held in New York in 1974, a strong English team was defeated 9–6 by the Americans. In the same year, 61 English players competed in the USDA's International Darts Classic. English players won the four-man team game but American players won the singles (George Silberzahn) and the doubles (Bob Thiede and Dan Valletto). At the end of this tournament, Ray Fischer from Philadelphia played Alan Evans in one game of "3001" for $2,000. Evans is regarded by many as currently the best player in Britain, but Fischer won using only 96 darts and averaging 94.7 per three-dart throw.

In the following year Conrad Daniels, then U.S. Champion, was invited to compete in England's Champion of Champions Tournament. He won this event, the first major tournament to be won by an American in England, despite the fact that he was competing against some of the finest players in the world.

Finally, it should be said that the national popularity of the game, combined with commercial promotion, has produced a growth within a few years that is probably unprecedented for any sport.

Tradition

Darts is a game of the people. To play, one does not have to join a special or exclusive club or invest in expensive equipment. Much of the game's character derives from its traditional home, the English pub, which is not merely a place to drink but a social institution.

The most important characteristic of the pub is that it is "local." To many, having a good local pub is as important an amenity as public transportation or shops. It is common to be asked, especially if you have recently moved, "What's your local like?" It is difficult to define a good "local." Certainly it means having good beer (about which much controversy rages among the experts). It also means a comfortable atmosphere without being pretentious. The ultimate test, however, is—is it friendly? Are you made to feel welcome? In a good local, the regular patrons, the landlord, and his staff know each other. They may indeed know each other very well but a certain decorum is exercised in pursuing private matters. The conversation may center on local gossip, sport, or the current political scandal. The pub is the people's equivalent of the rich men's club. It is an enclave where friendships can exist without the pressures of work or the obligations of domestic life.

It is in this atmosphere that the game of darts has flourished. The team, if the pub has one, will be both a local and a somewhat casual affair. It may compete with the Jolly Gardeners down the road or The King's Head some miles away, but it will be unlikely to travel out of its own area. The game will be played seriously with a desire to win. The rivalry may be intense, but the game is ultimately governed by a spirit of conviviality.

Of course, this is a somewhat idyllic picture, and there are aspects of the English pub that are less attractive. Visitors to England will be struck by the division of pubs into different sections, essentially reflecting the class system: the public bar, bare and simply furnished; the lounge or saloon, carpeted and plush; and the cocktail bar, catering to whatever brand of swinger happens to be in fashion. It is in the public bar—the working-class bar—that the dart board is to be found. Although working-class wives do go to the "public," it has traditionally been a male-dominated world. This no doubt accounts for the fact that, in the past, darts also has been very much a man's world. This is changing and ought to change. At the same time, it must be said that darts does not fit well into the atmosphere of pile carpets, plush, and cocktail chatter. The spirit of darts, its etiquette and language, have been formed by the ambience of the public bar. At its best it represents a democratic spirit, a world of ease and equality, friendliness and conviviality, that is a root part of the darts tradition.

Etiquette

Various unstated customs have grown up with the playing of darts. The simplest and most obvious is that each player retrieves his own darts. It is generally agreed that in a series of games the losers (the mugs) of the previous game throw first in the next; thus the expression "mugs away." In the traditional three-leg game of "301," sides will toss a coin or throw nearest the bull to see who throws first in the opening game; it is then mugs for the second game and, should a third be required, again a coin is tossed or a bull flung. Traditionally the score is kept on a blackboard although, unfortunately, in some American bars, paper is used, or nasty little plastic boards. Players entering a bar with a game in progress may indicate their desire to play by putting their initials on the blackboard. When the game in progress finishes, the newcomers then take over the scoring of the next—they "take the chalks," as the expression goes. When that game is complete the losers drop out (then "taking the chalks") and the new players enter the game. This arrangement prevents players from monopolizing the board for the entire evening. For someone on his own entering a strange bar the etiquette is more complicated. He will first get himself a beer and sit near the board to observe the game and betray interest. He may find himself a partner, in which case they can put their initials on the board, or if a game involving three players is in progress, he can offer to make up a fourth. If a singles game is in progress, however, he will be wise to observe for several games to assess both the skill of the players and the seriousness of the game. If the players are involved in intense competition at a higher level of skill than he is capable of, then he would be advised to remain for the moment an observer. If, however, he feels equal to them in skill, and they are merely indulging in a friendly game, he may then ask if he can take the chalks. Such an offer should be accepted. It is an important part of the game's tradition, allowing, as it does, for the stranger to enter the game and meet other players. Another important part of the game's etiquette is that a player should take the game seriously and pay attention to the scoring. Nothing is more irritating than the player who constantly drifts off from the game to have conversations in a different part of the bar and has to be called for his turn, not knowing what has been scored and what he must get.

It is very difficult to cheat at darts. Obviously players should not distract their opponents by talking loudly, dropping darts, etc., although players are used to throwing amidst the general conversation of the bar and absolute silence is not the rule. When a player retrieves his darts he should call out his score *before* removing the darts from the board. If darts have fallen close to a wire, then he should move those to one side with a finger, allowing his opponents to see clearly which bed they have entered. Apart from chalking up the wrong score, the only other way in which a player can gain advantage is by overstepping the hockey. The advantage gained is dubious and, indeed, the infraction is usually inadvertent. For the persistent offender, certain stock phrases are used to draw attention to his behavior. These have an ironic quality, which serves to maintain observance of the rules without being heavy-handed or pompous about it, and are usually uttered over the edge of a pint mug of beer and accompanied by a wink to the other players: "Wearing your father's boots, are you?" "You're getting your feet wet, Charlie." "Half-way for ladies, is it?"

Terminology

As already noted, darts, like other sports and social customs, has its own specialized language. Part of this language is self-evident, such as "double top" for double 20. Much of it derives from two sources. One of these is cockney rhyming slang, as in "On your knees," meaning two three's (double 3). The other is the language of bingo or, more properly, the same game called "Housey-housey" in the British Army and "Tombloa" in the Royal Navy. Some of the expressions are quite modern while others are ancient and obscene. As a matter of interest, we list some of these expressions below. However, readers should be warned that only relatively few are in common use; the visitor to an English pub who constantly called out "Annie's room" or "Swans on the lake" would be thought somewhat eccentric.

Annie's room: double 1, origin obscure.

Away: getting the opening double.

Bed: any wired-off segment of the board.

Bed and breakfast: getting 26 by scoring 20, 1, and 5. Originates in the fact that a long time ago 2/6 (two shillings and sixpence) was the cost of bed and breakfast for one night in a rooming house. (To indicate how darts terminology may have obscure origins, the 26 combination is called a Shafer in one Chicago pub, being named after an excellent player who has scored 26 more often than he would like.)

Bunghole: the bull, also called the cork.

Bust: scoring more than is required.

Clickety-click: 66.

Double top: 40.

Downstairs: the lower part of the board.

Front room: a close game, from the old saying "It's like our front room—nothing in it."

Game shot: the shot that wins the game.

Legs eleven: 11.

Lord Nelson: 111. Has reference to the legend that Lord Nelson was lacking three crucial organs, two of them being an eye and an arm.

Married man's side: numbers on the left side of the board (the safe area to throw for a reasonable score).

Middle for diddle: throw for nearest the bull to see who starts.

Mugs away: losers throw first.

Pair of plates: double eight.

Shanghai: when a player scores a single, double, and treble of the same number in one throw.

Split: when an odd number has to be broken down to leave a double. "Three to split" means you need one, double one to finish. Sometimes called "Three to crack."

Swans on the lake: 22.

Three in a bed: three darts in one segment.

Ton: 100. Also used in other combinations, such as ton-eighty for three treble 20s (180).

Two beehives: double five.

Two fleas: double three.

Two hens: double ten.

Upstairs: top of the board.

Whitewash: to have your opponent finish the game before you have got your opening double. Also called the brush, short for whitewash brush.

Drinks

Most dart players can, as they say, take a good drink. Many of them are, to use the English term, "piss artists." A look at the team pictures in *Darts World* will reveal a good proportion of "beer bellies." Darts is a splendid game, both stimulating and relaxing; but the most dedicated enthusiast could not make the claim for it that is made for other sports, i.e., that it is healthy exercise, tones up the muscles, keeps the figure trim, and fills the lungs with fresh air.

We have already suggested that a reasonable amount of drinking is an appropriate accompaniment to the game. This is not only, or even mainly, because of its supposed easing of tensions, which is less a physical fact than a mental effect, like Zen perhaps. Rather it is because the regular thrower will invariably play in the pub. After a good throw (or even a bad one) the player's hand will naturally move out to grasp his glass. For that glass not to be there would be as unnatural as for the scoreboard to be missing. Tom Barrett, the only player to win the *News of the World* Championship two years in succession, has recorded how at one stage of his career he decided not to drink before or during a game. He discovered that, rather than sharpen his game, this disruption of a lifetime habit produced a discordant sensation, a feeling of incongruity.

We have already warned about the dangers of overindulgence, of that exhilarating feeling of playing superbly when the scoreboard offers a flat contradiction. In this section we are concerned not with the question of how much to drink but with what to drink. The naive reader may, of course, feel that this is a matter of personal taste, but for those who have any respect for the traditions of the game this is not so.

Beer is the drink associated with darts. Classically it is a pint of draught. The basic wager for a game of "301" is to play for a pint. Some variation from this rule can be allowed. It would be an extremist who would impose foaming pints of draught on a lady with a small capacity for beer. Various lighter beers in smaller measures are allowable. In the English pub a drink called a Shandy is also quite permissible. This is a mixture, in equal proportions, of beer and lemonade (Seven-Up in America). This is a very refreshing drink, low in alcoholic content but effective in dissolving cigarette smoke and chalk dust without detracting from the aroma of that combination unique to the nostrils of the darts player. It also has the advantage of looking like beer, so that the addition of the degenerate Seven-Up is concealed from the onlooker, if not the drinker.

It is all a matter of style, a feel for tradition and an aesthetic sense. The solid shape of the beer mug, the light gold or mahogany brown of the liquid, not only fits the game but blends in with the proper decor and furniture of the darts bar. In the true darts bar, the furnishings are traditional materials like wood or brass, the colors burnt sienna and yellow ochre, the decorative element being provided by the glittering bottles and glasses. Into this scheme of things even the beer and nicotine stains blend.

Of course, traditions change and we would not wish to be rigid. Somewhat reluctantly we would be prepared to turn a blind eye to a player under stress who feels he must have a scotch and water or a lady who would rather have a gin and tonic than a beer. But there are limits, and certain standards must be maintained. Elaborate cocktails are out. There can be no place for the Tequila Sunrise, the Sloe Gin Fizz, or the Harvey Wallbanger in the darts bar. Such concoctions must be ruthlessly expelled to the cocktail lounge, where they belong with the plush, plastic, and pink, and the chatter of advertising executives and model girls.

The Old and the New

This chapter has been about the darts tradition, its social and cultural context and essentially democratic character. It has been about the past of darts. As such it has been written self-consciously, as archaic and nostalgic. A deliberately ideal world has been projected to sharpen the contrast between the old and the new, the new being phase three of the development of the modern game already described. This phase is very different from traditional pub darts with its casualness and camaraderie. It is a world of commercial sponsorship, tournaments, TV coverage, tournament stars with their agents, managers, and vociferous fans. New rules are imposed about dress; too casual wear is felt to be in bad taste and wrong for the image of darts. Prizes are more glittering and awards made by celebrities like Miss World supported by Playboy Bunnies and Penthouse Pets.

It is tempting for the British author of this jointly written book to attribute this to the Americans, to American drive, energy, organization, and commercial culture. In fact, it is part of a continuing process on both sides of the

Atlantic and, in the case of darts, it had its origins in England. Recently an English promoter of darts of the new school said he wanted to change the image of darts. "What we are trying to get away from," he said, "is the idea that darts consists of a lot of little blokes throwing arrows in a boozer." Leaving aside the patronizing adjective "little," this seems a reasonable description of the game. One cannot help having misgivings about this sort of thing.

Yet our feelings are inevitably mixed. Darts has always been a popular game even when played by a minority. By this we mean it is popular in the sense of being "of the people" in the same way that jazz music has been both popular and minority. It is now entering a phase in which it is becoming popular in the more usual sense, i.e., enjoyed and played by large numbers of people. A number of factors have led to this development and we would like to think that the game's intrinsic attraction was one. There is no doubt, however, that the main reason for this growth has been commercial promotion, tournament play, and star glamor. It would be bigoted not to welcome this development in the interests of some purist notion of the game. Indeed, we have to recognize that behind such a purism lies, not only a useless nostalgia, but an inverted snobbery that takes pride in being in touch with "the people" and esoteric pastimes. On the positive side we should note that similar developments in golf, for example, with big money tournaments and glamor stars like Nicklaus and Miller, have not, as far as one can see, undermined the pleasure of the 18-handicapper in his Sunday-morning game.

Still, it is worth making warning sounds. The promotion of darts is welcome if it brings pleasure to more people. But it must be a promotion that respects darts, its social roots and its traditions. It will only do damage to the game if it forgets that ultimately it is "a lot of little blokes throwing arrows in a boozer."

Appendix: Books

Books on darts are so few in number and generally so slight in content that the term *bibliography* would not be justified. None of the books listed casts any light on the origins of the game. As we have indicated in the text, the various books on games and pastimes make only passing reference to darts and, even at that, rarely to the modern game. To the best of our knowledge, no one is doing research in the history of darts.

The list below may be complete. When we began writing we thought we were producing the first book on the subject in America. That distinction must, however, go to Brackin and Fitzgerald. Apart from their book, all the others listed are English publications and mostly out of print. Of the modern books, Tom Barrett's is perhaps the most useful, and the pamphlet he worked on with Barry Twomlow for Unicorn provides precise and useful information. *The Watney Book of Pub Games* describes various games, many of them archaic. *The Indoor League* is a product of the English TV show of the same name, which is devoted to darts and other pub games.

Barrett, Tom. *Darts*. Pan Books, 1973.

Barrett, Tom and Barry Twomlow. *Darts: Rules, Equipment, and Technique*. Unicorn Products.

Brackin, I.L. and W. Fitzgerald. *All About Darts*. Double Top Publishing Co., 1975.

Caley, G. *How to Improve your Darts*. Photo Instruction Books, 1948.

Cooke, R.C. *Darts*. Bles, 1936.

D'Egville, A.H. & G. *Darts With the Lid Off*. Cassell, 1938.

Finn, Timothy. *The Watney Book of Pub Games*. Queen Anne Press, 1966.

Waddell, Sid and John Mead. *The Indoor League*. Pan Books, 1975.

Wellington, A. *Darts*. Universal Publications, 1937.

Williamson, Noel. *Darts*. Elliott Right Way Books, 1968.

Inn Games. (Know the Game Series). E P Publishing, Ltd.